International Library of Philosophy and Theology

BIBLICAL AND THEOLOGICAL STUDIES

J. Marcellus Kik, *Editor*

THE FIVE POINTS OF CALVINISM

Defined, Defended, Documented

DAVID N. STEELE

CURTIS C. THOMAS

THE FIVE POINTS OF

CALVINISM

DEFINED
DEFENDED
DOCUMENTED

by

David N. Steele
Curtis C. Thomas

Authors of
Romans: An Interpretive Outline

Preface by

Roger Nicole, Th. D.
Professor of Theology
Gordon Divinity School

Presbyterian & Reformed Publishing Co.
Box 817 — Phillipsburg, N.J. 08865

Parts I and II of this work have been published as an appendix to a larger work by
the authors entitled *Romans: An Interpretive Outline*

ISBN: 0-87552-444-3

Library of Congress Catalog Card Number 63-21695

Manufactured in the United States of America

It is with deep gratitude that we dedicate this book to

Loraine Boettner

in a p p r e c i a t i o n for his written m i n i s t r y, kind encouragement, and sacrificial Christian example.

PERMISSION TO QUOTE

PREFACE

Why another work on the *Five Points of Calvinism?* Is not the subject hackneyed and the division artificial? The writer of this preface has heard these objections and would like to address himself briefly to them.

It is true that there are a number of presentations of the five points of Calvinism. Some of them are of indifferent quality; others have outstanding merit. Some are of ancient vintage and have proven their worth in the passing of the decades. Others, of recent origin, are enriched through acquaintance with the previous literature on the subject. None, to the knowledge of the writer of this preface, sets out to do precisely what the present work aims to accomplish: to give a clear and concise definition of the Calvinistic position; to provide a conspectus of the Biblical foundation for each point; and to give a brief review of the literature available in English on the whole subject and on each point. To get this in compact form at a readily accessible price is certainly a most desirable project. Far from duplicating existing materials, this present work may be viewed as filling an unfortunate lacuna.

The second objection to be considered is that the division into the five points is not suited to give a proper representation of Calvinism. Several facets are left out, it is urged, and those that are present are not so clearly distinct as to warrant the strong emphasis upon the figure five. To be sure, this structure has its historical origin not in the harmonious internal self-development of Calvinism, but rather in the necessity to counter the objections of the Remonstrance (1610), which were formulated along five main heads of doctrine. Nevertheless, and in part, on account of these historical moorings, the five points provide a classic framework which is quite well adapted for the expression of certain distinguishing emphases of Calvinism. Furthermore, they are well suited for the exhibition of the inner correlation between Calvinistic tenets, since each of them may well be viewed as an aspect of the sovereign grace of God.

We do therefore welcome the present work as an added testimony to this great truth, and pray that, by its plain and lucid presentation, it will contribute to dispel misunderstandings and to forward "the cause of God and truth."

ROGER NICOLE

"It is no novelty, then, that I am preaching; no new doctrine. I love to proclaim these strong old doctrines, that are called by nickname CALVINISM, but which are surely and verily the revealed truth of God as it is in Christ Jesus. By this truth I make a pilgrimage into [the] past, and as I go, I see father after father, confessor after confessor, martyr after martyr, standing up to shake hands with me . . . . taking these things to be the standard of my faith, I see the land of the ancients peopled with my brethren; I behold multitudes who confess the same as I do, and acknowledge that this is the religion of God's own church."

Charles Haddon Spurgeon

INTRODUCTION

This work has been designed to serve as an *introductory survey* of that system of theology known as "the five points of Calvinism." As we shall see, each of the five points, which make up this historic system, constitutes a distinct and important Biblical doctrine. Viewed together, these five doctrines form the basic framework of God's plan for saving sinners.

The purpose of this survey is threefold: We wish first to *define*, second to *defend*, and third to *document* the "five points." In order to do this we have divided the material into three separate parts, each of which forms an independent unit of study.

Part One deals with the *history* and *contents* of the system. The sole function of this section is to explain what Calvinism is. In order to show how and why the five point structure of Calvinism was developed, we have discussed the origin and contents of "the five points of Arminianism." These two opposing systems are contrasted, point by point, so that it might be clearly understood wherein and to what extent they differ in their interpretation of the Biblical plan of salvation. The basic concepts of each system are analyzed, but no attempt whatsoever is made in Part One to defend the truthfulness of Calvinism.

Part Two is devoted to a *Biblical defense* of the five points of Calvinism. After each point has been introduced and related to the overall system, some of the more important verses in which it is taught are given. The various passages appealed to in the support of each point are classified under appropriate headings. Approximately 250 passages (consisting of well over 400 verses) are *quoted in full.*[1] Great care has been exercised to avoid quoting verses out of their context. Before considering the Biblical defense presented in Part Two, the reader should clearly understand the contents of Calvinism discussed in Part One.

Part Three is designed to *encourage* and *aid* the reader to make *a thorough investigation of Calvinistic theology.* We have *listed* and carefully *documented* (giving the author's full name, the title, the publisher's name and address, the date of publication, and the number of pages) *over 90 works* dealing with Calvinism and the individual doctrines contained within the system. Included in this list of titles are 60 separate books plus 15 reference works (systematic theologies, etc.), in addition to information concerning the Calvinistic contents of the great Protestant confessions of faith, and a number of booklets and tracts. Over 50 of

---

[1] All the Biblical quotations are from the *Revised Standard Version* of the Bible. The use of this version is not to be construed as a blanket endorsement, for it has its defects, especially in the Old Testament. Since all translations have their strengths as well as their weaknesses, we suggest that the verses quoted be checked in several translations. Among others, we recommend the *American Standard Version, The Berkeley Version, The Amplified New Testament, The New Testament: A Translation in the Language of the People* by Charles B. Williams, *Wuest's Expanded Translation of the Greek New Testament,* and *The New English Bible.*

the individual books (not including the reference works) are briefly introduced; we have indicated such things as the nature of their contents, their value, and their style. Many of these works have been written by the foremost theologians of both the past and present. They set forth and defend, explain and clarify, state and answer objections to, as well as show the influence and value of Calvinistic theology.[2]

It is our hope that the material contained in this survey will help to promote the spread of Calvinism and that many will thus be led to understand, to believe, and to propagate this Biblical system of doctrine—which ascribes *all the glory* for the salvation of sinners *to God alone!*

---

[2] Parts I and II of this work were first published as an appendix to *Romans: An Interpretive Outline*. These two parts, along with the material contained in Part III, are being published in this paperback edition in order to make it available at a more accessible price.

CONTENTS

CONTENTS—(Continued)

PART THREE—THE FIVE POINTS DOCUMENTED
Works Recommended for the Study of Calvinism

Section One
References Relating to the Overall Calvinistic System

Section Two
References Relating to Each of the "Five Points"

PART ONE

A BRIEF SURVEY OF THE ORIGIN AND CONTENTS OF THE "FIVE POINTS" OF CALVINISM

I. The Origin of the "Five Points"

To understand how and why the system of theology known to history as Calvinism came to bear this name and to be formulated into five points, one must understand the theological conflict which occurred in Holland during the first quarter of the seventeenth century.

A. The Protest of the Arminian Party

In 1610, just one year after the death of James Arminius (a Dutch seminary professor) *five articles of faith* based on his teachings were drawn up by his followers. The Arminians, as his followers came to be called, presented these five doctrines to the State of Holland in the form of a "Remonstrance" (i.e., a protest). The Arminian party insisted that the Belgic Confession of Faith and the Heidelberg Catechism (the official expression of the doctrinal position of the Churches of Holland) be changed to conform to the doctrinal views contained in the Remonstrance. The Arminians objected to those doctrines upheld in both the Catechism and the Confession relating to divine sovereignty, human inability, unconditional election or predestination, particular redemption, irresistible grace, and the perseverance of the saints. It was in connection with these matters that they wanted the official standards of the Church of Holland revised.

B. The "Five Points" of Arminianism

Roger Nicole summarizes the five articles contained in the Remonstrance as follows: "I. God elects or reproves on the basis of foreseen faith or unbelief. II. Christ died for all men and for every man, although only believers are saved. III. Man is so depraved that divine grace is necessary unto faith or any good deed. IV. This grace may be resisted. V. Whether all who are truly regenerate will certainly persevere in the faith is a point which needs further investigation."[3]

The last article was later altered so as to definitely teach the possibility of the truly regenerate believer's losing his faith and thus losing his salvation. Arminians however have not been in agreement on this point—some have held that all who are regenerated by the Spirit of God are eternally secure and can never perish.

---

[3] Roger Nicole, "Arminianism," *Baker's Dictionary of Theology*, p. 64.

C. The Philosophical Basis of Arminianism

J. I. Packer, in analyzing the system of thought embodied in the Remonstrance, observes, "The theology which it contained (known to history as Arminianism) stemmed from two philosophical principles: first, that divine sovereignty is not compatible with human freedom, nor therefore with human responsibility; second, that ability limits obligation . . . . From these principles, the Arminians drew two deductions: first, that since the Bible regards faith as a free and responsible act, it cannot be caused by God, but is exercised independently of Him; second, that since the Bible regards faith as obligatory on the part of all who hear the gospel, ability to believe must be universal. Hence, they maintained, Scripture must be interpreted as teaching the following positions: (1.) Man is never so completely corrupted by sin that he cannot savingly believe the gospel when it is put before him, nor (2.) is he ever so completely controlled by God that he cannot reject it. (3.) God's election of those who shall be saved is prompted by His foreseeing that they will of their own accord believe. (4.) Christ's death did not ensure the salvation of anyone, for it did not secure the gift of faith to anyone (there is no such gift) ; what it did was rather to create a possibility of salvation for everyone if they believe. (5.) It rests with believers to keep themselves in a state of grace by keeping up their faith; those who fail here fall away and are lost. Thus, Arminianism made man's salvation depend ultimately on man himself, saving faith being viewed throughout as man's own work and, because his own, not God's in him."[4]

D. The Rejection of Arminianism by the Synod of Dort and the Formation of the Five Points of Calvinism

A national Synod was called to meet in Dort in 1618 for the purpose of examining the views of Arminius in the light of Scripture. The Great Synod was convened by the States-General of Holland on November 13, 1618. There were 84 members and 18 secular commissioners. Included were 27 delegates from Germany, the Palatinate, Switzerland and England. There were 154 sessions held during the seven months that the Synod met to consider these matters, the last of which was on May 9, 1619.

"The Synod," Warburton writes, "had given a very close examination to the 'five points' which had been advanced by the Remonstrants, and had compared the teaching advanced in them with the testimony of Scripture. Failing to reconcile that teaching with the Word of God, which they had definitely declared could alone be accepted by them as the rule of faith, they had unanimously rejected them. They felt, however, that a mere rejection was not sufficient. It remained for them

---

[4] James I. Packer, "Introductory Essay," John Owen, *The Death of Death in the Death of Christ*, pp. 3, 4.

14

THE ORIGIN OF THE FIVE POINTS

to set forth the true Calvinistic teaching in relationship to those matters which had been called into question. This they proceeded to do, embodying the Calvinistic position in five chapters which have ever since been known as 'the five points of Calvinism.' "[5] The name *Calvinism* was derived from the great French reformer, John Calvin (1509-1564), who had done so much in expounding and defending these views.

No doubt it will seem strange to many in our day that the Synod of Dort rejected as heretical the five doctrines advanced by the Arminians, for these doctrines have gained wide acceptance in the modern Church. In fact, they are seldom questioned in our generation. But the vast majority of the Protestant theologians of that day took a much different view of the matter. They maintained that the Bible set forth a system of doctrine quite different from that advocated by the Arminian party. Salvation was viewed by the members of the Synod as *a work of grace from beginning to end;* in no sense did they believe that the sinner saved himself or contributed to his salvation. Adam's fall had completely ruined the race. All men were by nature spiritually dead and their wills were in bondage to sin and Satan. The ability to believe the gospel was itself a gift from God, bestowed only upon those whom He had chosen to be the objects of His unmerited favor. It was not man, but God, who determined which sinners would be shown mercy and saved. This, in essence, is what the members of the Synod of Dort understood the Bible to teach.

In the chart which follows, the five points of Arminianism (rejected by the Synod) and the five points of Calvinism (set forth by the Synod) are given, side by side, so that it might be readily seen wherein and to what extent these two systems of doctrine differ.

---

[5] Ben A. Warburton, *Calvinism*, p. 61. Although there were five Calvinistic Articles, there were only four chapters. This was because the third and fourth Articles were combined into one chapter. Consequently, the third chapter is always designated as Chapter III-IV.

II. The Five Points of Arminianism Contrasted with the Five Points of Calvinism

THE "FIVE POINTS" OF ARMINIANISM	THE "FIVE POINTS" OF CALVINISM
1. *Free Will or Human Ability*	1. *Total Inability or Total Depravity*
Although human nature was seriously affected by the fall, man has not been left in a state of total spiritual helplessness. God graciously enables every sinner to repent and believe, but He does so in such a manner as not to interfere with man's freedom. Each sinner possesses a free will, and his eternal destiny depends on how he uses it. Man's freedom consists of his ability to choose good over evil in spiritual matters; his will is not enslaved to his sinful nature. The sinner has the power to either cooperate with God's Spirit and be regenerated or resist God's grace and perish. The lost sinner needs the Spirit's assistance, but he does not have to be regenerated by the Spirit before he can believe, for faith is man's act and precedes the new birth. Faith is the sinner's gift to God; it is man's contribution to salvation.	Because of the fall, man is unable of himself to savingly believe the gospel. The sinner is dead, blind, and deaf to the things of God; his heart is deceitful a n d desperately corrupt. His will is not free, it is in bondage to his evil nature, therefore, he will not—indeed he cannot—choose good over evil in the spiritual r e a l m. Consequently, it takes much more than the Spirit's assistance to bring a s i n n e r to Christ—it takes regeneration by which the Spirit makes the sinner alive and gives him a new nature. Faith is not something man contributes to salvation but is itself a part of God's gift of salvation—it is God's gift to the sinner, not the sinner's gift to God.
2. *Conditional Election*	2. *Unconditional Election*
God's choice of certain individuals unto salvation before the foundation of the w o r l d was based upon His foreseeing that they would respond to His call. He selected only t h o s e	God's choice of certain individuals unto salvation before the foundation of the w o r l d rested solely in His own sovereign will. His choice of particular sinners was not based on

whom He knew would of themselves freely believe the gospel. Election therefore was determined by or conditioned upon what man would do. The faith which God foresaw and upon which He based His choice was not given to the sinner by God (it was not created by the regenerating power of the Holy Spirit) but r e s u l t e d solely from man's will. It was left entirely up to man as to who would believe and therefore as to who would be elected unto salvation. God c h o s e those whom He knew would, of their own free will, choose Christ. Thus the sinner's c h o i c e of Christ, not God's choice of the sinner, is the ultimate cause of salvation.

any foreseen response or obedience on their part, such as faith, repentance, etc. On the contrary, God gives faith and repentance to each individual whom He selected. These acts are the result, not the cause of God's choice. Election therefore was not determined by or conditioned upon any virtuous quality or act foreseen in man. Those whom God sovereignly elected He brings through the power of the Spirit to a willing acceptance of C h r i s t. Thus God's choice of the sinner, not the sinner's choice of Christ, is the ultimate cause of salvation.

3. *Universal Redemption or General Atonement*

C h r i s t's redeeming work made it possible for everyone to be saved but did not actually secure the salvation of anyone. Although Christ died for all men and for every man, only those who believe in Him are saved. His death enabled God to pardon sinners on the condition that they believe, but it did not actually put away anyone's sins. Christ's redemption becomes effective only if man chooses to accept it.

3. *Particular Redemption or Limited Atonement*

C h r i s t's redeeming work was intended to save the elect only and actually secured salvation for them. His death was a substitutionary endurance of the penalty of sin in the place of certain specified sinners. In addition to putting away the sins of His people, Christ's redemption secured everything necessary for their salvation, including faith which unites them to Him. The gift of faith is infallibly a p p l i e d by the Spirit to all for whom Christ died, t h e r e b y guaranteeing their salvation.

17

4. *The Holy Spirit Can Be Effectually Resisted*

The Spirit calls inwardly all those who are called outwardly by the gospel invitation; He does all that He can to bring every sinner to salvation. But inasmuch as man is free, he can successfully r e s i s t the Spirit's call. The Spirit cannot regenerate the sinner until he believes; faith (which is man's contribution) precedes a n d makes possible the new birth. Thus, man's free will limits the Spirit in the application of Christ's s a v i n g work. The Holy Spirit can only draw to Christ those who allow Him to have His way with them. Until the s i n n e r responds, the Spirit cannot give life. God's grace, therefore, is not invincible; it can be, and often is, resisted and thwarted by man.

4. *The Efficacious Call of the Spirit or Irresistible Grace*

In addition to the outward general call to salvation which is made to everyone who hears the gospel, the Holy Spirit extends to the elect a special inward call that i n e v i t a b l y brings them to salvation. The external call (which is made to all without distinction) can be, and often is, rejected; whereas the i n t e r n a l call (which is made only to the elect) cannot be rejected; it always results in conversion. By means of this special call the Spirit irresistibly draws s i n n e r s to Christ. He is not limited in His work of applying salvation by man's will, nor is He dependent upon man's cooperation for success. The S p i r i t graciously causes the elect sinner to cooperate, to believe, to repent, to come freely and willingly to Christ. God's grace, therefore, is invincible; it never fails to result in the salvation of those to whom it is extended.

5. *Falling from Grace*

Those who believe and are truly saved can lose their salvation by failing to keep up their faith, etc.

All Arminians have not been agreed on this p o i n t; some have held that believers are eternally secure in Christ— that once a sinner is regenerated, he can never be lost.

5. *Perseverance of the Saints*

All who were chosen by God, redeemed by Christ, and given faith by the Spirit are eternally s a v e d. They are kept in faith by the p o w e r of Almighty God and thus persevere to the end.

18

According to Arminianism:

Salvation is a c c o m p l i s h e d through the combined efforts of *God* (who takes the initiative) and *man* (who must respond)—man's response being the determining factor. God has provided salvation for everyone, but His provision becomes effective only for those who, of their own free will, "choose" to cooperate with Him and accept His offer of grace. At the crucial point, man's will plays a decisive role; thus *man*, not God, determines who will be the recipients of the gift of salvation.

According to Calvinism:

Salvation is accomplished by the almighty power of the Triune God. The Father chose a people, the Son died for them, the Holy Spirit makes Christ's death effective by bringing the elect to faith and repentance, thereby causing them to willingly obey the gospel. The entire process (election, redemption, regeneration) is the work of God and is by grace alone. Thus *God*, not man, determines who will be the recipients of the gift of salvation.

REJECTED
by the Synod of Dort

This was the system of thought contained in the "Remonstrance" (though the "five points" were not originally arranged in this order). It was submitted by the Arminians to the Church of Holland in 1610 for adoption but was rejected by the Synod of Dort in 1619 on the ground that it was unscriptural.

REAFFIRMED
by the Synod of Dort

This system of theology was reaffirmed by the Synod of Dort in 1619 as the doctrine of salvation contained in the Holy Scriptures. The system was at that time formulated into "five points" (in answer to the five points submitted by the Arminians) and has ever since been known as "the five points of Calvinism."

III. The Basic Concepts of Each System Are Much Older Than the Synod of Dort

A. The Controversy between Pelagius and Augustine

Neither John Calvin nor James Arminius originated the basic concepts which undergird the two systems that bear their names. The fundamental principles of each system can be traced back many centuries prior to the time when these two men lived. For example, the basic doctrines of the Calvinistic position had been vigorously defended by Augustine against Pelagius during the fifth century. Cunningham writes, "As there was nothing new in substance in the Calvinism of Calvin, so there was nothing new in the Arminianism of Arminius; . . . . The doctrines of Arminius can be traced back as far as the time of Clemens Alexandrinus, and seem to have been held by many of the fathers of the third and fourth centuries, having been diffused in the church through the corrupting influence of pagan philosophy. Pelagius and his followers, in the fifth century, were as decidedly opposed to Calvinism as Arminius was, though they deviated much further from sound doctrine than he did."[6]

Pelagius denied that human nature had been corrupted by sin. He maintained that the only ill effects which the race had suffered as the result of Adam's transgression was the bad example which he had set for mankind. According to Pelagius, every infant comes into the world in the same condition as Adam was before the fall. His leading principle was that *man's will is absolutely free.* Hence every one has the power, within himself, to believe the gospel as well as to perfectly keep the law of God.

Augustine, on the other hand, maintained that human nature had been so completely corrupted by Adam's fall that no one, in himself, has the ability to obey either the law or the gospel. Divine grace is essential if sinners are to believe and be saved, and this grace is extended only to those whom God predestined to eternal life before the foundation of the world. The act of faith, therefore, results, not from the sinner's free will (as Pelagius taught) but from God's free grace which is bestowed on the elect only.

B. Semi-Pelagianism, the Forerunner of Arminianism

Smeaton, in showing how Semi-Pelagianism (the forerunner of Arminianism) originated, states that "Augustin's unanswerable polemic had so fully discredited Pelagianism in the field of argument, that it could no longer be made plausible to the Christian mind. It collapsed. But a new system soon presented itself, teaching that *man with his own natural powers is able to take the first step toward his conversion,* and that this obtains or merits the Spirit's assistance. Cassian . . . was the founder of this middle way, which came to be called SEMI-PELAGIAN-ISM, because it occupied intermediate ground between Pelagianism and Augustinianism, and took in elements from both. He acknowledged that Adam's sin extended to his posterity, and that human nature was corrupted by original sin. But, on the other hand, he held a system of universal grace for all men alike, making the final decision in the case of every individual dependent on the exercise of free-will." Speaking of those who followed Cassian, Smeaton continues, "they held that the first movement of the will in the assent of faith must be ascribed to the natural powers of the human mind. This was their primary error. Their maxim was: '*it is mine to be willing* to believe, and it is the part of God's grace to assist.' They asserted the sufficiency of Christ's grace for all, and that every one, according to his own will, obeyed or rejected the invitation, while God equally wished and equally aided all men to be saved . . . . The entire system thus formed is a half-way house containing elements

---

* William Cunningham, *Historical Theology*, Vol. II, p. 374.

of error and elements of truth, and not at all differing from the Arminianism which, after the resuscitation of the doctrines of grace by the Reformers, diffused itself in the very same way through the different Churches."[7]

C. Calvinism, the Theology of the Reformation

The leaders of the Protestant Reformation of the sixteenth century rejected Pelagianism and Semi-Pelagianism on the ground that both systems were unscriptural. Like Augustine, the Reformers held to the doctrines of the sovereignty of God, the total depravity of man, and of unconditional election. As Boettner shows, they stood together in their view of predestination. "It was taught not only by Calvin, but by Luther, Zwingli, Melancthon (although Melancthon later retreated toward the Semi-Pelagian position), by Bullinger, Bucer, and all of the outstanding leaders in the Reformation. While differing on some other points they agreed on this doctrine of Predestination and taught it with emphasis. Luther's chief work, 'The Bondage of the Will,' shows that he went into the doctrine as heartily as did Calvin himself."[8]

Packer states that "all the leading Protestant theologians of the first epoch of the Reformation, stood on precisely the same ground here. On other points, they had their differences; but in asserting the helplessness of man in sin, and the sovereignty of God in grace, they were entirely at one. To all of them, these doctrines were the very life-blood of the Christian faith . . . . To the Reformers, the crucial question was not simply, whether God justifies believers without works of law. It was the broader question, whether sinners are wholly helpless in their sin, and whether God is to be thought of as saving them by free, unconditional, invincible grace, not only justifying them for Christ's sake when they come to faith, but also raising them from the death of sin by His quickening Spirit in order to bring them to faith. Here was the crucial issue: whether God is the author, not merely of justification, but also of faith; whether, in the last analysis, Christianity is a religion of utter reliance on God for salvation and all things necessary to it, or of self-reliance and self-effort."[9]

---

[7] George Smeaton, *The Doctrine of the Holy Spirit*, pp. 300, 301. Italics and capitalizations are his. Semi-Pelagianism was repudiated by the Synod of Orange in 529 A. D., just as Arminianism was repudiated by the Synod of Dort almost eleven hundred years later.

[8] Loraine Boettner, *The Reformed Doctrine of Predestination*, p. 1.

[9] James I. Packer and O. R. Johnston, "Historical and Theological Introduction," Martin Luther, *Bondage of the Will*, pp. 58, 59. In speaking of the English Reformation, Buis shows that "the advocates of that Reformation were definitely Calvinistic." To substantiate this he quotes the following from Fisher, " 'The Anglican Church agreed with the Protestant Churches on the continent on the subject of predestination. On this subject, for a long period, the Protestants generally were united in opinion.' 'The leaders of the English Reformation, from the time when the death of Henry VIII placed them firmly upon Protestant ground, profess the doctrine of absolute as distinguished from conditional predestination.' " Harry Buis, *Historic Protestantism and Predestination*, p. 87.

Thus it is evident that the five points of Calvinism, drawn up by the Synod of Dort in 1619, was by no means a new system of theology. On the contrary, as Dr. Wyllie asserts of the Synod, "It met at a great crisis and it was called to review, re-examine and authenticate over again, in the second generation since the rise of the Reformation, that body of truth and system of doctrine which that great movement had published to the world."[10]

IV. The Difference between Calvinism and Arminianism

The issues involved in this historic controversy are indeed grave, for they vitally affect the Christian's concept of God, of sin, and of salvation. Packer, in contrasting these two systems, is certainly correct in asserting that "The difference between them is not primarily one of emphasis, but of content. One proclaims a God Who saves; the other speaks of a God Who enables man to save himself. One view [Calvinism] presents the three great acts of the Holy Trinity for the recovering of lost mankind—election by the Father, redemption by the Son, calling by the Spirit—as directed towards the same persons, and as securing their salvation infallibly. The other view [Arminianism] gives each act a different reference (the objects of redemption being all mankind, of calling, those who hear the gospel, and of election, those hearers who respond), and denies that any man's salvation is secured by any of them. The two theologies thus conceive the plan of salvation in quite different terms. One makes salvation depend on the work of God, the other on a work of man; one regards faith as part of God's gift of salvation, the other as man's own contribution to salvation; one gives all the glory of saving believers to God, the other divides the praise between God, Who, so to speak, built the machinery of salvation, and man, who by believing operated it. Plainly, these differences are important, and the permanent value of the 'five points,' as a summary of Calvinism, is that they make clear the points at which, and the extent to which, these two conceptions are at variance."[11]

V. The *One Point* Which the "Five Points" of Calvinism Are Concerned to Establish

While recognizing the permanent value of the five points as a summary of Calvinism, Packer warns against simply equating Calvinism with the five points. He gives several excellent reasons why such an equation is incorrect, one of which we quote: ". . . the very act of setting

---

[10] Quoted by Warburton, *Calvinism*, p. 58. Smeaton says of the work of the Synod of Dort that "it may be questioned whether anything more valuable as an ecclesiastical testimony for the doctrines of sovereign, special, efficacious grace was ever prepared on this important theme since the days of the apostles." George Smeaton, *The Doctrine of the Holy Spirit*, p. 320.

[11] Packer, "Introductory Essay," (above, fn. 4), pp. 4,5.

out Calvinistic soteriology [the doctrine of salvation] in the form of five distinct points (a number due, as we saw, merely to the fact that there were five Arminian points for the Synod of Dort to answer) tends to obscure the organic character of Calvinistic thought on this subject. For the five points, though separately stated, are really inseparable. They hang together; you cannot reject one without rejecting them all, at least in the sense in which the Synod meant them. For to Calvinism there is really only *one* point to be made in the field of soteriology: the point that *God saves sinners. God*—the Triune Jehovah, Father, Son and Spirit; three Persons working together in sovereign wisdom, power and love to achieve the salvation of a chosen people, the Father electing, the Son fulfilling the Father's will by redeeming, the Spirit executing the purpose of Father and Son by renewing. *Saves*—does everything, first to last, that is involved in bringing man from death in sin to life in glory: plans, achieves and communicates redemption, calls and keeps, justifies, sanctifies, glorifies. *Sinners*—men as God finds them, guilty, vile, helpless, powerless, unable to lift a finger to do God's will or better their spiritual lot. *God saves sinners*—and the force of this confession may not be weakened by disrupting the unity of the work of the Trinity, or by dividing the achievement of salvation between God and man and making the decisive part man's own, or by soft-pedalling the sinner's inability so as to allow him to share the praise of his salvation with his Saviour. This is the one point of Calvinistic soteriology which the 'five points' are concerned to establish and Arminianism in all its forms to deny: namely, that sinners do not save themselves in any sense at all, but that salvation, first and last, whole and entire, past, present and future, is of the Lord, to whom be glory for ever; amen."[12]

This brings to completion Part One of our survey. No attempt whatsoever has been made in this section to prove the truthfulness of the Calvinistic doctrines. Our sole purpose has been to give a brief history of the system and to explain its contents. We are now ready to consider its Biblical support.

---

[12] Packer, "Introductory Essay," (above, fn. 4), p. 6. Italics are his.

PART TWO
BIBLICAL SUPPORT FOR THE "FIVE POINTS" OF CALVINISM

The question of supreme importance is not how the system under consideration came to be formulated into five points, or why it was named Calvinism, but rather *is it supported by Scripture?* The final court of appeal for determining the validity of any theological system is the inspired, authoritative Word of God. If Calvinism can be verified by clear and explicit declarations of Scripture, then it must be received by Christians; if not, it must be rejected. For this reason, Biblical passages are given below in support of the five points.

After each point has been introduced, some of the more important verses in which it is taught are quoted. All quotations are from the *Revised Standard Version* of the Bible. In each case, the italics within the verses are ours. Apart from the remarks contained in the headings under which the verses are given, there are no explanatory comments as to their meaning. This procedure was necessary because of the limited design of this introductory survey. To compensate for this, we have recommended a number of works in Part Three which deal with these as well as with many other passages of Scripture related to Calvinism.

Although the "five points" are dealt with below under separate headings, and texts are classified in support of each of them individually, they must not be evaluated on a purely individual basis. For these five doctrines are not presented in the Bible as separate and independent units of truth. On the contrary, in the Biblical message they are woven into one harmonious, interrelated system in which God's plan for recovering lost sinners is marvelously displayed. In fact, these doctrines are so inseparably connected that no one of them can be fully appreciated unless it is properly related to, and viewed in light of the other four; for *they mutually explain and support one another.* To judge these doctrines individually without relating each to the others would be like attempting to evaluate one of Rembrandt's paintings by looking at only one color at a time and never viewing the work as a whole. Do not, therefore, merely judge the Biblical evidence for each point separately, but rather consider carefully the collective value of the evidence when these five doctrines are viewed together as a system. When thus properly correlated, they form a fivefold cord of unbreakable strength.

I. TOTAL DEPRAVITY OR TOTAL INABILITY

The view one takes concerning salvation will be determined, to a large extent, by the view one takes concerning sin and its effects on human nature. It is not surprising, therefore, that the first article dealt with in the Calvinistic system is the Biblical doctrine of total inability or total depravity.

When Calvinists speak of man as being totally depraved, they mean that man's nature is corrupt, perverse, and sinful throughout. The adjective "total" does not mean that each sinner is as totally or completely corrupt in his actions and thoughts as it is possible for him to be. Instead, the word "total" is used to indicate that the *whole* of man's being has been affected by sin. The corruption extends to *every part* of man, his body and soul; sin has affected all (the totality) of man's faculties—his mind, his will, etc.

As a result of this inborn corruption, the natural man is totally unable to do anything spiritually good; thus Calvinists speak of man's "total inability." The inability intended by this terminology is *spiritual inability;* it means that the sinner is so spiritually bankrupt that *he can do nothing pertaining to his salvation.* It is quite evident that many unsaved people, when judged by man's standards, do possess admirable qualities and do perform virtuous acts. But in the spiritual realm, when judged by God's standards, the unsaved sinner is incapable of good. The natural man is enslaved to sin; he is a child of Satan, rebellious toward God, blind to truth, corrupt, and unable to save himself or to prepare himself for salvation. In short, the unregenerate man is DEAD IN SIN, and his WILL IS ENSLAVED to his evil nature.

Man did not come from the hands of his Creator in this depraved, corrupt condition. God made Adam upright; there was no evil whatsoever in his nature. Originally, Adam's will was free from the dominion of sin; he was under no natural compulsion to choose evil, but through his fall he brought spiritual death upon himself and all his posterity. He thereby plunged himself and the entire race into spiritual ruin and lost for himself and his descendants the ability to make right choices in the spiritual realm. His descendants are still free to choose—every man makes choices throughout life—but inasmuch as Adam's offspring are born with sinful natures, they do not have the ABILITY to choose spiritual good over evil. Consequently, man's will is no longer free (i.e., free from the dominion of sin) as Adam's will was free before the fall. Instead, man's will, as the result of inherited depravity, is in bondage to his sinful nature.

The Westminster Confession of Faith gives a clear, concise statement of this doctrine. "Man, by his fall into a state of sin, hath wholly lost all ability of will to any spiritual good accompanying salvation; so as a natural man, being altogether averse from good, and dead in sin, is not able, by his own strength, to convert himself, or to prepare himself thereunto."[13]

A. As the result of Adam's transgression, men are born in sin and by nature are spiritually dead; therefore, if they are to become God's children and enter His kingdom, they must be born anew of the Spirit.

---

[13] Chapter IX, Section 3.

PART II: THE FIVE POINTS DEFENDED

1. When Adam was placed in the garden of Eden, he was warned not to eat the fruit of the tree of knowledge of good and evil on the threat of immediate *spiritual* death.

   Genesis 2:16,17: And the Lord God commanded the man, saying, "You may freely eat of every tree of the garden; but of the tree of the knowledge of good and evil you shall not eat, for in the day that you eat of it you shall *die*."

2. Adam disobeyed and ate of the forbidden fruit (Genesis 3:1-7); consequently, he brought spiritual death upon himself and upon the race.

   Romans 5:12: Therefore as sin came into the world through one man [Adam, see vs. 14] and *death* through sin, and so death spread to all men because all men sinned.

   Ephesians 2:1-3: And you he *made alive*, when you were *dead* through the trespasses and sins in which you once walked, following the course of this world, following the prince of the power of the air, the spirit that is now at work in the sons of disobedience. Among these we all once lived in the passions of our flesh, following the desires of body and mind, and so we were *by nature* children of wrath, like the rest of mankind.

   Colossians 2:13: And you, who were *dead* in trespasses and the uncircumcision of your flesh, *God made alive* together with him, having forgiven us all our trespasses.

3. David confessed that he, as well as all other men, was born in sin.

   Psalm 51:5: Behold, I was brought forth in iniquity, and in sin did my mother conceive me.

   Psalm 58:3: The wicked go astray from the womb, they err from their birth, speaking lies.

4. Because men are born in sin and are by nature spiritually dead, Jesus taught that men must be born anew if they are to enter God's kingdom.

   John 3:5-7: Jesus answered, "Truly, truly, I say to you, unless one is born of water and the Spirit, he cannot *enter* the kingdom of God. That which is born of the flesh is flesh, and that which is born of the Spirit is spirit. Do not marvel that I said to you, '*You must be born anew.*' " Compare John 1:12,13.

26

B. As the result of the fall, men are blind and deaf to spiritual truth. Their minds are darkened by sin; their hearts are corrupt and evil.

Genesis 6:5: The Lord saw that the wickedness of man was great in the earth, and that *every imagination of the thoughts of his heart was only evil continually.*

Genesis 8:21: . . . the imagination of man's heart is *evil* from his youth . . .

Ecclesiastes 9:3: . . . the *hearts* of men are *full of evil*, and madness is in their hearts while they live . . .

Jeremiah 17:9: The *heart* is *deceitful above all things,* and *desperately corrupt;* who can understand it?

Mark 7:21-23: "For from within, *out of the heart of man,* come evil thoughts, fornication, theft, murder, adultery, coveting, wickedness, deceit, licentiousness, envy, slander, pride, foolishness. All these evil things come from within, and they defile a man."

John 3:19: And this is the judgment, that the light has come into the world, and *men loved darkness* rather than light, because their deeds were evil.

Romans 8:7,8: For the *mind* that is set on the flesh is hostile to God; *it* does not submit to God's law, indeed *it cannot;* and those who are in the flesh *cannot please God.*

I Corinthians 2:14: The unspiritual man does not receive the gifts of the Spirit of God, for they are folly to him, and *he is not able to understand them* because they are spiritually discerned.

Ephesians 4:17-19: Now this I affirm and testify in the Lord, that you must no longer live as the Gentiles do, in the futility of their minds; they are *darkened in their understanding,* alienated from the life of God because of the ignorance that is in them, *due to their hardness of heart;* they have become callous and have given themselves up to licentiousness, greedy to practice every kind of uncleanness.

Ephesians 5:8: For once you were *darkness,* but now you are light in the Lord . . .

Titus 1:15: To the pure all things are pure, but to the corrupt and unbelieving nothing is pure; *their very minds and consciences are corrupted.*

C. Before sinners are born into God's kingdom through the regenerating power of the Spirit, they are children of the devil and under his control; they are slaves to sin.

John 8:44: You are of *your father the devil,* and *your will* is to do your father's desires.

Ephesians 2:1,2: And you he made alive, when you were dead through the trespasses and sins in which you once walked, following the course of this world, *following the prince of the power of the air,* the spirit that is now at work in the sons of disobedience.

II Timothy 2:25,26: God may perhaps grant that they will repent and come to know the truth, and they may escape from *the snare of the devil,* after being *captured by him to do his will.*

I John 3:10: By this it may be seen who are the children of God, and who are the *children of the devil:* whoever does not do right is not of God, nor he who does not love his brother.

I John 5:19: We know that we are of God, and the whole world is *in the power of the evil one.*

John 8:34: Jesus answered them, "Truly, truly, I say to you, every one who commits sin is *a slave to sin."*

Romans 6:20: When you were *slaves of sin,* you were free in regard to righteousness.

Titus 3:3: For we ourselves were once foolish, disobedient, led astray, *slaves* to various passions and pleasures, passing our days in malice and envy, hated by men and hating one another.

D. The reign of sin is universal; all men are under its power; consequently, none is righteous—not even one!

II Chronicles 6:36: . . . for there is *no man* who does not sin . . . Compare I Kings 8:46.

Job 15:14-16: What is man, that he can be clean? Or he that is born of a woman, that he can be righteous? Behold, God puts no trust in his holy ones, and the heavens are not clean in his sight; how much less one who is abominable and corrupt, a man who drinks iniquity like water!

Psalm 130:3: If thou, O Lord, shouldst mark iniquities, Lord, *who could stand?*

Psalm 143:2: Enter not into judgment with thy servant; for no *man living* is righteous before thee.

Proverbs 20:9: *Who* can say, "I have made my heart clean; I am pure from my sin"?

Ecclesiastes 7:20: Surely there is *not a righteous man on earth* who does good and never sins.

Ecclesiastes 7:29: Behold, this alone I found, that God made man upright, but they have sought out many devices.

Isaiah 53:6: All we like sheep have gone astray; we have turned every one to his own way. . .

Isaiah 64:6: We have all become like one who is unclean, and all our righteous deeds are like a polluted garment. We all fade like a leaf, and our iniquities, like the wind, take us away.

Romans 3:9-12: What then? Are we Jews any better off? No, not at all; for I have already charged that *all men*, both Jews and Greeks, *are under the power of sin*, as it is written; "None is righteous, no, not one; no one understands, no one seeks for God. All have turned aside, together they have gone wrong; *no one does good, not even one.*"

James 3:2,8: For we all make many mistakes, and if any one makes no mistakes in what he says he is a perfect man, able to bridle the whole body also . . . . but no human being can tame the tongue—a restless evil, full of deadly poison.

I John 1:8,10: If we say we have no sin, we deceive ourselves, and the truth is not in us . . . . If we say we have not sinned, we make him a liar, and his word is not in us.

E. Men left in their dead state are unable of themselves to repent, to believe the gospel, or to come to Christ. They have no power within themselves to change their natures or to prepare themselves for salvation.

Job 14:4: Who can bring a clean thing out of an unclean? There is not one.

Jeremiah 13:23: Can the Ethiopian change his skin or the leopard his spots? Then also you can do good who are accustomed to do evil.

Matthew 7:16-18: You will know them by their fruits. Are grapes gathered from thorns, or figs from thistles? So, every sound tree bears good fruit, but the bad tree bears evil fruit. A sound tree cannot bear evil fruit, *nor can a bad tree bear good fruit.*

Matthew 12:33: "Either make the tree good, and its fruit good; or make the tree bad, and its fruit bad; for the tree is known by its fruit."

John 6:44: *No one can come to me unless* the Father who sent me *draws him;* and I will raise him up at the last day.

John 6:65: And he said, "This is why I told you that *no one can come to me unless it is granted him* by the Father."

Romans 11:35,36: "Or *who has given a gift to him* that he might be repaid?" For *from him* and through him and to him *are all things.* To him be glory forever. Amen.

I Corinthians 2:14: The *unspiritual man* does not receive the gifts of the Spirit of God, for they are folly to him, and *he is not able to understand them* because they are spiritually discerned.

I Corinthians 4:7: For who sees *anything different in you?* What have you that you did not receive? If then you received it, *why do you boast as if it were not a gift?*

II Corinthians 3:5: Not that we are *sufficient of ourselves* to claim anything as coming from us; our sufficiency is *from God.*

For further Biblical confirmation that men are unable of themselves to do anything toward gaining salvation, see the Scriptures given below under Point IV on Efficacious Grace. Note especially those verses which state that GOD *gives* faith, *grants* repentance, *creates* a new heart within the sinner, and other similar expressions.

II. UNCONDITIONAL ELECTION

Because of Adam's transgression, his descendants enter the world as guilty, lost sinners. As fallen creatures, they have no desire to have fellowship with the Creator. He is holy, just, and good, whereas they are sinful, perverse, and corrupt. Left to their own choices, they inevitably follow the god of this world and do the will of their father, the devil. Consequently, men have cut themselves off from the Lord of heaven and have forfeited all rights to His love and favor. It would have been perfectly just for God to have left all men in their sin and misery and to have shown mercy to none. God was under no obligation whatsoever to provide salvation for anyone. It is in this context that the Bible sets forth the doctrine of election.

The doctrine of election declares that God, before the foundation of the world, chose certain individuals from among the fallen members of Adam's race to be the objects of His undeserved favor. These, and these only, He purposed to save. God could have chosen to save all men (for He had the power and authority to do so) or He could have chosen to save none (for He was under no obligation to show mercy to any)—but He did neither. Instead He chose to save some and to exclude others. His eternal choice of particular sinners unto salvation was not based upon any foreseen act or response on the part of those selected, but was based solely on His own good pleasure and sovereign will. Thus election was not determined by, or conditioned upon, anything that men would do, but resulted entirely from God's self-determined purpose.

Those who were not chosen to salvation were passed by and left to their own evil devices and choices. It is not within the creature's jurisdiction to call into question the justice of the Creator for not choosing every one to salvation. It is enough to know that the Judge of the earth has done right. It should, however, be kept in mind that if God had not graciously *chosen* a people for Himself and sovereignly determined to *provide* salvation for them and *apply* it to them, none would be saved. The fact that He did this for some, to the exclusion of others, is in no way unfair to the latter group, unless of course one maintains that God was under obligation to provide salvation for sinners—a position which the Bible utterly rejects.

The doctrine of election should be viewed not only against the backdrop of human depravity and guilt, but it should also be studied in connection with the *eternal covenant* or agreement made between the members of the Godhead. For it was in the execution of this covenant that the *Father* chose out of the world of lost sinners a definite number of individuals and gave them to the Son to be His people. The *Son,* under the terms of this compact, agreed to do all that was necessary to save those "chosen" and "given" to Him by the Father. The *Spirit's* part in the execution of this covenant was to apply to the elect the salvation secured for them by the Son.

Election, therefore, is but *one* aspect (though an important aspect) of the saving purpose of the Triune God, and thus must not be viewed *as* salvation. For the act of election *itself* saved no one; what it did was to mark out certain individuals for salvation. Consequently, the doctrine of election must not be divorced from the doctrines of human guilt, redemption, and regeneration or else it will be distorted and misrepresented. In other words, if it is to be kept in its proper Biblical balance and correctly understood, *the Father's act of election* must be related to the *redeeming work of the Son* who gave Himself to save the elect and to the *renewing work of the Spirit* who brings the elect to faith in Christ!

A. General statements showing that God has an elect people, that He predestined them to salvation, and thus to eternal life.

> Deuteronomy 10:14,15: Behold, to the Lord your God belong heaven and the heaven of heavens, the earth with all that is in it; yet *the Lord set his heart in love* upon your fathers and *chose* their descendants after them, you above all peoples, as at this day.

> Psalm 33:12: Blessed is the nation whose God is the Lord, the people whom he has *chosen* as his heritage!

31

Psalm 65:4: Blessed is he whom thou dost *choose* and bring near, to dwell in thy courts! We shall be satisfied with the goodness of thy house, thy holy temple!

Psalm 106:5: . . . that I may see the prosperity of thy *chosen ones,* that I may rejoice in the gladness of thy nation, that I may glory with thy heritage.

Haggai 2:23: "On that day, says the Lord of hosts, I will take you, O Zerubbabel my servant, the son of Shealtiel, says the Lord, and make you like a signet ring; for I have *chosen* you, says the Lord of hosts."

Matthew 11:27: ". . . no one knows the Father except the Son and any one to whom the Son *chooses* to reveal him."

Matthew 22:14: "For many are called, but few are *chosen.*"

Matthew 24:22,24,31: And if those days had not been shortened, no human being would be saved; but for the sake of the *elect* those days will be shortened . . . . For false Christs and false prophets will arise and show great signs and wonders, so as to lead astray, if possible, even *the elect* . . . . and he will send out his angels with a loud trumpet call, and they will gather *his elect* from the four winds, from one end of heaven to the other.

Luke 18:7: And will not God vindicate *his elect,* who cry to him day and night?

Romans 8:28-30: We know that in everything God works for good with those who love him, who are *called according to his purpose.* For those whom he foreknew he also *predestined* to be conformed to the image of his Son, in order that he might be the first-born among many brethren. And those whom he predestined he also called; and those whom he called he also justified; and those whom he justified he also glorified.

Romans 8:33: Who shall bring any charge against *God's elect?*

Romans 11:28: As regards the gospel they are enemies of God, for your sake; but as regards *election* they are beloved for the sake of their forefathers.

Colossians 3:12: Put on then, as *God's chosen ones,* holy and beloved, compassion, kindness, . . .

I Thessalonians 5:9.: For God has not *destined* us for wrath, *but to obtain salvation* through our Lord Jesus Christ.

Titus 1:1: Paul, a servant of God and an apostle of Jesus Christ, to further the faith of *God's elect* and their knowledge of the truth which accords with godliness . . .

I Peter 1:1,2: To the exiles of the dispersion . . . *chosen* and *destined* by God the Father and sanctified by the Spirit for obedience to Jesus Christ and for sprinkling with his blood . . .

I Peter 2:8,9: . . . for they stumble because they disobey the word, as they were *destined* to do. But you are a *chosen* race, a royal priesthood, a holy nation, God's own people, that you may declare the wonderful deeds of him who *called* you out of darkness into his marvelous light.

Revelation 17:14: "They will make war on the Lamb, and the Lamb will conquer them, for he is Lord of lords and King of kings, and those with him are *called* and *chosen* and faithful."

B. Before the foundation of the world, God chose particular individuals unto salvation. His selection was *not based upon any foreseen response or act* performed by those chosen. Faith and good works are the *result*, not the *cause* of God's choice.

1. God did the choosing.

Mark 13:20: And if the Lord had not shortened the days, no human being would be saved; but for the sake of *the elect, whom he chose,* he shortened the days.

See also I Thessalonians 1:4 and II Thessalonians 2:13 quoted below.

2. God's choice was made before the foundation of the world.

Ephesians 1:4: Even as he *chose* us in him *before the foundation of the world,* that we should be holy and blameless before him:

See II Thessalonians 2:13; II Timothy 1:9; Revelation 13:8 and Revelation 17:8 quoted below.

3. God chose particular individuals unto salvation—their names were written in the book of life before the foundation of the world.

Revelation 13:8: And all who dwell on earth will worship it, every one whose *name* has not been *written before the foundation of the world* in the book of life of the Lamb that was slain.

Revelation 17:8: ". . . and the dwellers on earth whose *names* have not been *written* in the book of life *from the foundation of the world,* will marvel to behold the beast, because it was and is not and is to come."

4. God's choice was not based upon any forseen merit residing in those whom He chose, nor was it based on any foreseen good works performed by them.

> Romans 9:11-13: Though they were *not yet born and had done nothing either good or bad,* in order that God's purpose of *election* might continue, *not because of works* but because of his *call,* she was told, "The elder will serve the younger." As it is written, "Jacob I loved, but Esau I hated."

> Romans 9:16: So it depends *not upon man's will or exertion,* but upon *God's mercy.*

> Romans 10:20: ". . . I have been found by those who did not seek me; I have shown myself to those who did not ask for me."

> I Corinthians 1:27-29: *God chose* what is *foolish* in the world to shame the wise, *God chose* what is *weak* in the world to shame the strong, *God chose* what is *low and despised* in the world, even things that are not, to bring to nothing things that are, *so that no human being might boast in the presence of God.*

> II Timothy 1:9: . . . who saved us and called us with a holy calling, not in virtue of *our works* but in virtue of *his own purpose* and the *grace* which he gave us in Christ Jesus *ages ago.*

5. Good works are the result, not the ground, of predestination.

> Ephesians 1:12: We who first hoped in Christ have been *destined* and *appointed* to live for the praise of his glory.

> Ephesians 2:10: For we are his workmanship, created in Christ Jesus *for good works,* which *God prepared beforehand,* that we should walk in them.

> John 15:16: You did not choose me, but *I chose you* and *appointed you* that you should go and bear fruit and that your fruit should abide; so that whatever you ask the Father in my name, he may give it to you.

6. God's choice was not based upon foreseen faith. Faith is the result and therefore the evidence of God's election, not the cause or ground of His choice.

> Acts 13:48: And when the Gentiles heard this, they were glad and glorified the word of God; and as many as were *ordained* to eternal life *believed.*

> Acts 18:27: . . . he greatly helped those who *through grace had believed.*

Philippians 1:29: For it has been *granted* to you that for the sake of Christ you should not only *believe* in him but also suffer for his sake.

Philippians 2:12,13: Therefore, my beloved, as you have always obeyed, so now, not only as in my presence but much more in my absence, work out your own salvation with fear and trembling; *for God is at work in you, both to will and to work for his good pleasure.*

I Thessalonians 1:4,5: For *we know*, brethren beloved by God, that *he has chosen you; for our gospel came to you* not only in word, but also *in power* and *in the Holy Spirit* and *with full conviction.*

II Thessalonians 2:13,14: ... *God chose you from the beginning to be saved, through* sanctification by the Spirit and *belief in the truth.* To this he called you through our gospel, so that you may obtain the glory of our Lord Jesus Christ.

James 2:5: ... Has not *God chosen* those who are poor in the world *to be rich in faith* and *heirs of the kingdom* which he has promised to those who love him?

See the Appendix on The Meaning of "Foreknew" in Romans 8:29. See also those verses quoted below under Point IV on Efficacious Grace, which teach that faith and repentance are the gifts of God and are wrought in the soul by the regenerating power of the Holy Spirit.

7. It is by faith and good works that one confirms his calling and election.

II Peter 1:5-11: For this very reason make every effort to supplement your faith with virtue, and virtue with knowledge, and knowledge with self-control, and self-control with steadfastness, and steadfastness with godliness, and godliness with brotherly affection, and brotherly affection with love. For if these things are yours and abound, they keep you from being ineffective or unfruitful in the knowledge of our Lord Jesus Christ. For whoever lacks these things is blind and shortsighted and has forgotten that he was cleansed from his old sins. Therefore, brethren, be the more zealous *to confirm your call and election,* for if you do this you will never fall; so there will be richly provided for you an entrance into the eternal kingdom of our Lord and Savior Jesus Christ.

C. Election is not salvation but is *unto* salvation. Just as the president-elect does not become the president of the United States *until* he is inaugurated, those chosen unto salvation are not saved *until* they are regenerated by the Spirit and justified by faith in Christ.

Romans 11:7: What then? Israel failed to obtain what it sought. *The elect obtained it,* but the rest were hardened.

II Timothy 2:10: Therefore I endure everything for the sake of *the elect,* that they also *may obtain the salvation* which in Christ Jesus goes with eternal glory.

See Acts 13:48; I Thessalonians 1:4 and II Thessalonians 2:13, 14 quoted above. Compare Ephesians 1:4 with Romans 16:7. In Ephesians 1:4 Paul shows that men were *chosen* "in Christ" before the world began. From Romans 16:7 it is clear that men are not *actually* "in Christ" until their conversion.

D. Election was based on the sovereign, distinguishing mercy of Almighty God. It was not man's will but God's will that determined which sinners would be shown mercy and saved.

Exodus 33:19: ". . . I will be gracious to whom I will be gracious, and will show mercy on whom I will show mercy."

Deuteronomy 7:6,7: "For you are a people holy to the Lord your God; the Lord your God has chosen you to be a people for his own possession, out of all the peoples that are on the face of the earth. It was not because you were more in number than any other people that the Lord set his love upon you and chose you, for you were the fewest of all peoples."

Matthew 20:15: " 'Am I not allowed to do what I choose with what belongs to me?' . . ."

Romans 9:10-24: And not only so, but also when Rebecca had conceived children by one man, our forefather Isaac, though they were not yet born and had done nothing either good or bad, in order that God's purpose of election might continue, not because of works but because of his call, she was told, "the elder will serve the younger." As it is written, "Jacob I loved, but Esau I hated." What shall we say then? Is there injustice on God's part? By no means! For he says to Moses, *"I will have mercy on whom I have mercy and I will have compassion on whom I have compassion."* So it depends not upon man's will or exertion, *but upon God's mercy.* For the Scripture says to Pharaoh, "I have raised you up for the very purpose of showing my power in you, so that my name may be proclaimed in all the earth." So then he has mercy *upon whomever he wills,* and

36

he hardens the heart of whomever he wills. You will say to me then, "Why does he still find fault? For who can resist his will?" But, who are you, a man, to answer back to God? Will what is molded say to its molder, "Why have you made me thus?" *Has the potter no right over the clay*, to make out of the same lump one *vessel for beauty* and another for menial use? What if God, desiring to show his wrath and to make known his power, has endured with much patience the vessels of wrath made for destruction, in order to make known the riches of his glory for the *vessels of mercy, which he has prepared beforehand for glory*, even us whom he has called, not from the Jews only but also from the Gentiles?

Romans 11:4-6: But what is God's reply to him? "I have kept for myself seven thousand men who have not bowed the knee to Baal." So too at the present time there is a remnant, *chosen by grace*. But if it is by grace, it is no longer on the basis of works; otherwise grace would no longer be grace. Compare I Kings 19:10, 18.

Romans 11:33-36: O the depth of the riches and wisdom and knowledge of God! How unsearchable are his judgments and how inscrutable his ways! "For who has known the mind of the Lord, or who has been his counselor?" "Or who has given a gift to him that he might be repaid?" For from him and through him and to him are all things. To him be glory for ever. Amen.

Ephesians 1:5: He destined us in love to be his sons through Jesus Christ, according to the purpose of his will.

E. The doctrine of election is but a part of the much broader Biblical doctrine of God's absolute sovereignty. The Scriptures not only teach that God predestined certain individuals unto eternal life, but that all events, both small and great, come about as the result of God's eternal decree. The Lord God rules over heaven and earth with absolute control; nothing comes to pass apart from His eternal purpose.

I Chronicles 29:10-12: Therefore David blessed the Lord in the presence of all the assembly; and David said: "Blessed art thou, O Lord, the God of Israel our father, for ever and ever. Thine, O Lord, is the greatness, and the power, and the glory, and the victory, and the majesty; for all that is in the heavens and in the earth is thine; thine is the kingdom, O Lord, and thou art exalted as head above all. Both riches and honor come from thee, and thou rulest over all. In thy hand are power and might; and in thy hand it is to make great and to give strength to all."

Job 42:1,2: Then Job answered the Lord: "I know that thou canst do all things, and that no purpose of thine can be thwarted."

Psalm 115:3: Our God is in the heavens; he does whatever he pleases.

Psalm 135:6: Whatever the Lord pleases he does, in heaven and on earth, in the seas and all deeps.

Isaiah 14:24,27: The Lord of hosts has sworn: "As I have planned, so shall it be, and as I have purposed, so shall it stand .... For the Lord of hosts has purposed, and who will annul it? His hand is stretched out, and who will turn it back?"

Isaiah 46:9-11: "Remember the former things of old; for I am God, and there is no other; I am God, and there is none like me, declaring the end from the beginning and from ancient times things not yet done, saying, 'My counsel shall stand, and I will accomplish all my purpose, calling a bird of prey from the east, the man of my counsel from a far country. I have spoken, and I will bring it to pass; I have purposed, and I will do it.' "

Isaiah 55:11: "So shall my word be that goes forth from my mouth; it shall not return to me empty, but it shall accomplish that which I purpose, and prosper in the things for which I sent it."

Jeremiah 32:17: " 'Ah Lord God! It is thou who hast made the heavens and the earth by thy great power and by thy outstretched arm! Nothing is too hard for thee.' "

Daniel 4:35: All the inhabitants of the earth are accounted as nothing; and he does according to his will in the host of heaven and among the inhabitants of the earth; and none can stay his hand or say to him, "What doest thou?"

Matthew 19:26: ". . . with God all things are possible."

III. PARTICULAR REDEMPTION OR LIMITED ATONEMENT

As was observed above, election itself saved no one; it only marked out particular sinners for salvation. Those *chosen* by the Father and given to the Son had to be *redeemed* if they were to be saved. In order to secure their redemption, Jesus Christ came into the world and took upon Himself human nature so that He might identify Himself with His people and act as their legal representative or substitute. Christ, acting on behalf of His people, perfectly kept God's law and thereby worked out a perfect righteousness which is imputed or credited to them the moment they are brought to faith in Him. Through what He did, they are constituted righteous before God. They are also freed from all guilt and condemnation as the result of what Christ suffered for them. Through His substitutionary sacrifice He endured the penalty of their sins and thus removed their guilt forever. Consequently, when His people are joined to Him by faith, they are credited with perfect righteousness and are freed from all guilt and condemnation. They are saved, not because of what they themselves have done or will do, but solely on the ground of Christ's redeeming work.

Historical or main line Calvinism has consistently maintained that Christ's redeeming work was definite in *design* and *accomplishment*— that it was intended to render complete satisfaction for certain specified sinners and that it actually secured salvation for these individuals and for no one else. The salvation which Christ earned for His people includes everything involved in bringing them into a right relationship with God, including the gifts of faith and repentance. Christ did not die simply to make it possible for God to pardon sinners. Neither does God leave it up to sinners as to whether or not Christ's work will be effective. On the contrary, all for whom Christ sacrificed Himself will be saved infallibly. Redemption, therefore, was designed to bring to pass God's purpose of election.

All Calvinists agree that Christ's obedience and suffering were of infinite value, and that if God had so willed, the satisfaction rendered by Christ would have saved every member of the human race. It would have required no more obedience, nor any greater suffering for Christ to have secured salvation for every man, woman, and child who ever lived than it did for Him to secure salvation for the elect only. But He came into the world to represent and save only those given to Him by the Father. Thus Christ's saving work was limited in that it was designed to save some and not others, but it was not limited in value for it was of infinite worth and would have secured salvation for everyone if this had been God's intention.

The Arminians also place a limitation on the atoning work of Christ, but one of a much different nature. They hold that Christ's saving work was designed to make possible the salvation of all men on the condition that they believe, but that Christ's death *in itself* did not actually secure or guarantee salvation for anyone.

Since all men will not be saved as the result of Christ's redeeming work, a limitation must be admitted. Either the atonement was limited in that it was *designed to secure* salvation for certain sinners but not for others, or it was limited in that it was not intended to secure salvation for any, but was *designed only to make it possible* for God to pardon sinners on the condition that they believe. In other words, one must limit its design either in *extent* (it was not intended for all) or *effectiveness* (it did not secure salvation for any). As Boettner so aptly observes, for the Calvinist, the atonement "is like a narrow bridge which goes all the way across the stream; for the Arminian it is like a great wide bridge that goes only half-way across."[14]

A. The Scriptures describe the end intended and accomplished by Christ's work as the full salvation (actual reconciliation, justification, and sanctification) of His people.

1. The Scriptures state that Christ came, not to enable men to save themselves, but to *save* sinners.

   Matthew 1:21: ". . . she will bear a son, and you shall call his name Jesus, for he will *save his people* from their sins."

   Luke 19:10: "For the Son of man came to seek and to *save* that which was lost."

   II Corinthians 5:21: For our sake he [God] made him [Christ] to be sin who knew no sin, so that in him *we might become* the righteousness of God.

   Galatians 1:3,4: Grace to you and peace from God the Father and our Lord Jesus Christ, *who gave himself* for our sins *to deliver us* from the present evil age, according to the will of our God and Father.

   I Timothy 1:15: The saying is sure and worthy of full acceptance, that Christ Jesus came into the world to *save* sinners. And I am the foremost of sinners.

   Titus 2:14: . . . who *gave himself* for us to *redeem us* from all iniquity and to purify for himself a people of his own who are zealous for good deeds.

---

[14] Boettner, *Predestination*, p. 153. Spurgeon's comments, as to whether it is the Calvinists or the Arminians who limit the atonement, are to the point. "We are often told that we limit the atonement of Christ, because we say that Christ has not made a satisfaction for all men, or all men would be saved. Now, our reply to this is, that, on the other hand, our opponents limit it: we do not. The Arminians say, Christ died for all men. Ask them what they mean by it. Did Christ die so as to secure the salvation of all men? They say, 'No, certainly not.' We ask them the next question—Did Christ die so as to secure the salvation of any man in particular? They answer 'No.' They are obliged to admit this, if they are consistent. They say, 'No. Christ has died that any man may be saved if'—and then follow certain conditions of salvation. Now, who is it that limits the death of Christ? Why, you. You say that Christ did not die so as infallibly to secure the salvation of anybody. We beg your pardon, when you say we limit Christ's death; we say, 'No, my dear sir, it is you that do it.' We say Christ so died that he infallibly secured the salvation of a multitude that no man can number, who through Christ's death not only may be saved, but are saved and cannot by any possibility run the hazard of being anything but saved. You are welcome to your atonement; you may keep it. We will never renounce ours for the sake of it." Quoted from Packer, "Introductory Essay," (above, fn. 4), p. 14.

I Peter 3:18: For *Christ* also *died* for sins once for all, the righteous for the unrighteous, *that he might bring us to God,* being put to death in the flesh but made alive in the spirit.

2. The Scriptures declare that, as the result of what Christ did and suffered, His people are reconciled to God, justified, and given the Holy Spirit who regenerates and sanctifies them. All these blessings were secured by Christ Himself for His people.

   a. Christ, by His redeeming work, secured *reconciliation* for His people.

      Romans 5:10: For if while we were enemies we were *reconciled* to God *by the death of his Son,* much more, now that we are reconciled, shall we be saved by his life.

      II Corinthians 5:18,19: All this is from God, who through Christ *reconciled* us to himself and gave us the ministry of reconciliation; that is, God was in Christ reconciling the world to himself, not counting their trespasses against them, and entrusting to us the message of reconciliation.

      Ephesians 2:15,16: ... by abolishing in his flesh the law of commandments and ordinances, that he might create in himself one new man in place of the two, so making peace, and *might reconcile us* both to God in one body through the cross, thereby bringing the hostility to an end.

      Colossians 1:21,22: And you, who once were estranged and hostile in mind, doing evil deeds, *he has now reconciled* in his body of flesh by his death, *in order to* present you holy and blameless and irreproachable before him.

   b. Christ secured the righteousness and pardon needed by His people for their *justification.*

      Romans 3:24,25: ... they are *justified* by his grace as a gift, *through the redemption which is in Christ Jesus,* whom God put forward as an expiation by his blood, to be received by faith. This was to show God's righteousness, because in his divine forbearance he had passed over former sins.

      Romans 5:8,9: But God shows his love for us in that *while we were yet sinners Christ died for us.* Since, therefore, we are now *justified by his blood,* much more shall we be saved by him from the wrath of God.

I Corinthians 1:30: He is the source of your life in Christ Jesus, whom God made our wisdom, our *righteousness* and sanctification and redemption.

Galatians 3:13: Christ *redeemed us* from the curse of the law, having become a curse for us . . .

Colossians 1:13,14: He has delivered us from the dominion of darkness and transferred us to the kingdom of his beloved Son, in whom *we have redemption,* the forgiveness of sins.

Hebrews 9:12: . . . he entered once for all into the Holy Place, *taking* not the blood of goats and calves but *his own blood, thus securing an eternal redemption.*

I Peter 2:24: He himself *bore our sins* in his body on the tree, that we might die to sin and live to righteousness. By his wounds you have been healed.

c. Christ secured the gift of the Spirit which includes *regeneration* and *sanctification* and all that is involved in them.

Ephesians 1:3,4: Blessed be the God and Father of our Lord Jesus Christ, who has blessed us in Christ *with every spiritual blessing* in the heavenly places, even as he chose us in him before the foundation of the world, that we should be holy and blameless before him.

Philippians 1:29: For it has been *granted to you* that for the sake of Christ you should not only *believe* in him but also suffer for his sake.

Acts 5:31: "God exalted him at his right hand as Leader and Savior, *to give repentance* to Israel and forgiveness of sins."

Titus 2:14: . . . who gave himself for us to *redeem us* from all iniquity and *to purify* for himself a people of his own who are zealous for good deeds.

Titus 3:5,6: . . . he saved us, not because of deeds done by us in righteousness, but in virtue of his own mercy, by the washing of *regeneration* and *renewal* in the Holy Spirit, which he poured out upon us richly *through* Jesus Christ our Savior.

Ephesians 5:25,26: Husbands, love your wives, as Christ loved the church and gave himself up for her, that he might *sanctify* her, having cleansed her by the washing of water with the word.

I Corinthians 1:30: He is the source of your life in Christ Jesus, whom God made our wisdom, our righteousness and *sanctification* and redemption.

Hebrews 9:14: ... how much more shall the *blood of Christ*, who through the eternal Spirit offered himself without blemish to God, *purify* your conscience from dead works to serve the living God.

Hebrews 13:12: So Jesus also *suffered* outside the gate *in order to sanctify* the people through his own blood.

I John 1:7: ... but if we walk in the light, as he is in the light, we have fellowship with one another, and the *blood of Jesus* his Son *cleanses* us from all sin.

B. Passages which represent the Lord Jesus Christ, in all that He did and suffered for His people, as fulfilling the terms of a gracious compact or arrangement which He had entered into with His heavenly Father before the foundation of the world.

1. Jesus was sent into the world by the Father to save the people which the Father had given to Him. Those given to Him by the Father come to Him (see and believe in Him) and none of them shall be lost.

John 6:35-40: Jesus said to them, "I am the bread of life; he who comes to me shall not hunger, and he who believes in me shall never thirst. But I said to you that you have seen me and yet do not believe. *All that the Father gives me will come to me;* and him who comes to me I will not cast out. For I have come down from heaven, not to do my own will, but *the will of him who sent me;* and this is the will of him who sent me, *that I should lose nothing of all that he has given me,* but raise it up at the last day. For this is the will of my Father, that every one who sees the Son and believes in him should have eternal life; and I will raise him up at the last day."

2. Jesus, as the good shepherd, lays down His life for His sheep. All who are "His sheep" are brought by Him into the fold and are made to hear His voice and follow Him. Notice that the Father had given the sheep to Christ!

John 10:11,14-18: "I am the good shepherd. The good shepherd lays down his life for *the sheep* .... I am the good shepherd; *I know my own* and my own know me, as the Father knows me and I know the Father; and I lay down my life for *the sheep.* And I have *other sheep*, that are not of this fold; *I must bring them also,* and they *will* heed my voice.

43

So there shall be one flock, one shepherd. **For this reason** the Father loves me, because I lay down my life, **that I** may take it again. No one takes it from me, but I lay it down of my own accord. I have power to lay it down, and I have power to take it again; *this charge I have received from my Father*."

John 10:24-29: [The unbelieving Jews demanded of Him] "If you are the Christ, tell us plainly." Jesus answered them, "I told you, and you do not believe. The works that I do in my Father's name, they bear witness to me; but you do not believe, *because you do not belong to my sheep*. *My sheep hear my voice*, and *I know them*, and *they* follow me; and *I give them eternal life*, and *they* shall never perish, and no one shall snatch *them* out of my hand. My *Father, who has given them to me*, is greater than all, and no one is able to snatch *them* out of the Father's hand."

3. Jesus, in His high priestly prayer, prays not for the world but for those given to Him by the Father. In fulfillment of the Father's charge Jesus had accomplished the work the Father had sent Him to do—to make God known to His people and to give them eternal life.

John 17:1-11, 20, 24-26: When Jesus had spoken these words, he lifted up his eyes to heaven and said, "Father, the hour has come; glorify thy Son that the Son may glorify thee, *since thou hast given him power over all flesh, so that he might give eternal life to all whom thou hast given him*. And this is eternal life, that they know thee the only true God, and *Jesus Christ whom thou hast sent*. I glorified thee on earth, having *accomplished the work which thou gavest me to do;* and now, Father, glorify thou me in thy own presence with the glory which I had with thee *before the world was made*.

"I have *manifested thy name to the men whom thou gavest me out of the world;* thine they were, and thou gavest them to me, and they have kept thy word. Now they know that everything that thou hast given me is from thee; for I have given them the words which thou gavest me, and they have received them and know in truth that I came from thee; and they have believed that thou didst send me. I am praying for them; *I am not praying for the world but for those whom thou hast given me*, for they are thine; all mine are thine, and thine are mine, and I am glorified in them. And now I am no more in the world, but they are in the world, and I am coming to thee. Holy Father, *keep them* in thy name *which thou hast given me,* that they may be one, even as we are one . . . . I do not pray for these only, but *also for those who are to believe in me* through their word, . . . Father, I desire that they also, *whom thou hast given me,* may be with me where I am, to behold my glory which thou hast given me in thy love for me *before the foundation of the world.* O righteous Father, the world has not known thee, but I have known thee; and *these know that thou hast sent me.* I made known to them thy name, and I will make it known, that the love with which thou hast loved me may be in them, and I in them."

4. Paul declares that all of the "spiritual blessings" which the saints inherit such as sonship, redemption, the forgiveness of sin, etc., result from their being "in Christ," and he traces these blessings back to their ultimate source in the eternal counsel of God—to that great blessing of their having been chosen in Christ before the foundation of the world and destined to be God's sons through Him.

Ephesians 1:3-12: Blessed be the God and Father of our Lord Jesus Christ, *who has blessed us* in Christ *with every spiritual blessing* in the heavenly places, *even as he chose us in him before the foundation of the world,* that we should be holy and blameless before him. He *destined us* in love *to be his sons through Jesus Christ, according to the purpose of his will,* to the praise of his glorious grace which he freely bestowed on us in the Beloved. In him we have *redemption* through his blood, *the forgiveness of our trespasses,* according to the riches of his grace which he lavished upon us. For he has made known to us in all wisdom and insight the mystery of his will, according to his purpose which he set forth in Christ as a plan for the fullness of time, to unite all things in him, things in heaven and things on earth.

In him, *according to the purpose of him who accomplishes all things according to the counsel of his will,* we who first hoped in Christ have been destined and appointed to live for the praise of his glory.

5. The parallel which Paul draws between the condemning work of Adam and the saving work of Jesus Christ the "second man," the "last Adam," can best be explained on the principle that both stood in covenant relation to "their people" (Adam stood as the federal head of the race, and Christ stood as the federal head of the elect). As Adam involved his people in death and

45

condemnation by his sin, even so Christ brought justification and life to His people through His righteousness.

Romans 5:12,17-19: Therefore as sin came into the world through one man [Adam] and death through sin, and so death spread to all men because all men sinned . . . . If, because of one man's trespass, death reigned through that one man, much more will those who receive the abundance of grace and the free gift of righteousness reign in life through the one man Jesus Christ. Then as one man's trespass led to condemnation for all men, so *one man's act of righteousness leads to acquittal and life for all men.* For as by one man's disobedience many were made sinners, so *by one man's obedience many will be made righteous.*

C. Some passages speak of Christ's dying for "all" men and of His death as saving the "world," yet others speak of His death as being definite in design and of His dying for particular people and securing salvation for them.

1. There are two classes of texts that speak of Christ's saving work in *general terms:* (a) Those containing the word "world"— e.g., John 1:9,29; 3:16,17; 4:42; II Corinthians 5:19; I John 2:1,2; 4:14 and (b) Those containing the word "all"—e.g., Romans 5:18; II Corinthians 5:14,15; I Timothy 2:4-6; Hebrews 2:9; II Peter 3:9.

One reason for the use of these expressions was to correct the false notion that salvation was for the Jews alone. Such phrases as "the world," "all men," "all nations," and "every creature" were used by the New Testament writers to emphatically correct this mistake. These expressions are intended to show that Christ died for all men without *distinction* (i.e., He died for Jews and Gentiles alike) but they are not intended to indicate that Christ died for all men without *exception* (i.e., He did not die for the purpose of saving each and every lost sinner).

2. There are other passages which speak of His saving work in *definite terms* and show that it was intended to infallibly save a particular people, namely those given to Him by the Father.

Matthew 1:21: ". . . for he will save *his people* from their sins."

Matthew 20:28: ". . . the Son of man came not to be served but to serve, and to give his life as *a ransom for many.*"

Matthew 26:28: ". . . for this is my blood of the covenant, which is poured out *for many* for the forgiveness of sins."

John 10:11: "I am the good shepherd. The good shepherd lays down his life for *the sheep*."

John 11:50-53: ". . . you do not understand that it is expedient for you that one man should die for *the people,* and not that the whole nation should perish." He did not say this of his own accord, but being high priest that year he prophesied that Jesus should die for the nation, and not for the nation only, but to gather into one *the children of God who are scattered abroad.* So from that day on they took counsel how to put him to death.

Acts 20:28: Take heed to yourselves and to all the flock, in which the Holy Spirit has made you guardians, to feed *the church* of the Lord *which he obtained for himself with his own blood.*

Ephesians 5:25-27: Husbands, love your wives, *as Christ loved the church* and *gave himself up for her,* that he might sanctify *her,* having cleansed *her* by the washing of water with the word, that *the church* might be presented before him in splendor, without spot or wrinkle or any such thing, that *she* might be holy and without blemish.

Romans 8:32-34: He who did not spare his own Son but gave him up *for us all,* will he not also *give* us all things with him? Who shall bring any charge against *God's elect?* It is God who justifies; who is to condemn?

Hebrews 2:17; 3:1: Therefore he had to be made like his brethren in every respect, so that he might become a merciful and faithful high priest in the service of God, to make expiation *for the sins of the people* . . . . Therefore, holy brethren, *who share in a heavenly call,* consider Jesus, the apostle and high priest of our confession.

Hebrews 9:15: Therefore he is the mediator of a new covenant, so that *those who are called* may receive the promised eternal inheritance, since a death has occurred which *redeems them* from the transgressions under the first covenant.

Hebrews 9:28: . . . Christ, having been offered once to bear the sins of *many* . . .

Revelation 5:9: . . . and they sang a new song, saying, "Worthy art thou to take the scroll and to open its seals, for thou wast slain and by thy blood didst *ransom men* for God *from every tribe and tongue and people and nation* . . ."

Review also the verses quoted above under B, 1, 2, 3.

47

PART II: THE FIVE POINTS DEFENDED

IV. THE EFFICACIOUS CALL OF THE SPIRIT OR IRRESISTIBLE GRACE

Each member of the Trinity—the Father, the Son, and the Holy Spirit—participates in and contributes to the salvation of sinners. As was shown above, the Father, before the foundation of the world, marked out those who were to be saved and gave them to the Son to be His people. At the appointed time the Son came into the world and secured their redemption. But these two great acts—election and redemption—do not complete the work of salvation, because included in God's plan for recovering lost sinners is the renewing work of the Holy Spirit by which the benefits of Christ's obedience and death are applied to the elect. It is with this phase of salvation (its application by the Spirit) that the doctrine of Irresistible or Efficacious Grace is concerned. Simply stated, this doctrine asserts that the Holy Spirit never fails to bring to salvation those sinners whom He personally calls to Christ. He inevitably applies salvation to every sinner whom He intends to save, and it is His intention to save all the elect.

The *gospel invitation extends a call* to salvation to every one who hears its message. It invites all men without distinction to drink freely of the water of life and live. It promises salvation to all who repent and believe. But this outward general call, extended to the elect and non-elect alike, will not bring sinners to Christ. Why? Because men are by nature dead in sin and are under its power. They are of themselves unable and unwilling to forsake their evil ways and to turn to Christ for mercy. Consequently, the unregenerate will not respond to the gospel call to repentance and faith. No amount of external threatenings or promises will cause blind, deaf, dead, rebellious sinners to bow before Christ as Lord and to look to Him alone for salvaticn. Such an act of faith and submission is contrary to the lost man's nature.

Therefore, the *Holy Spirit,* in order to bring God's elect to salvation, extends to them *a special inward call* in addition to the outward call contained in the gospel message. Through this special call the Holy Spirit performs a work of grace within the sinner which inevitably brings him to faith in Christ. The inward change wrought in the elect sinner enables him to understand and believe spiritual truth; in the spiritual realm he is given the seeing eye and the hearing ear. The Spirit creates within him a new heart or a new nature. This is accomplished through regeneration or the new birth by which the sinner is made a child of God and is given spiritual life. His will is renewed through this process so that the sinner spontaneously comes to Christ of his own free choice. Because he is given a new nature so that he loves righteousness, and because his mind is enlightened so that he understands and believes the Biblical gospel, the renewed sinner freely and willingly turns to Christ as Lord and Saviour.

48

Thus the once dead sinner is drawn to Christ by the inward supernatural call of the Spirit who through regeneration makes him alive and creates within him faith and repentance.

Although the general outward call of the gospel can be, and often is, rejected, the special inward call of the Spirit never fails to result in the conversion of those to whom it is made. This special call is not made to all sinners but is issued to the elect only! The Spirit is in no way dependent upon their help or cooperation for success in His work of bringing them to Christ. It is for this reason that Calvinists speak of the Spirit's call and of God's grace in saving sinners as being "efficacious," "invincible," or "irresistible." For the grace which the Holy Spirit extends to the elect cannot be thwarted or refused, it never fails to bring them to true faith in Christ!

The doctrine of Irresistible or Efficacious Grace is set forth in the Westminster Confession of Faith in the following words. "All those whom God hath predestinated unto life, and those only, he is pleased, in his appointed and accepted time, effectually to call, by his word and Spirit, out of that state of sin and death in which they are by nature, to grace and salvation by Jesus Christ; enlightening their minds spiritually and savingly to understand the things of God; taking away their heart of stone, and giving unto them an heart of flesh; renewing their wills, and by his almighty power determining them to that which is good, and effectually drawing them to Jesus Christ; yet so as they come most freely, being made willing by his grace."[15]

A. General statements showing that salvation is the work of the Spirit as well as that of the Father and the Son.

Romans 8:14: For all who are led by the Spirit of God are sons of God.

I Corinthians 2:10-14: For the Spirit searches everything, even the depths of God. For what person knows a man's thoughts except the spirit of the man which is in him? So also no one comprehends the thoughts of God except the Spirit of God. Now we have received not the spirit of the world, but the Spirit which is from God, that we might understand the gifts bestowed on us by God. And we impart this in words not taught by human wisdom but taught by the Spirit, interpreting spiritual truths to those who possess the Spirit.

I Corinthians 6:11: But you were washed, you were sanctified, you were justified in the name of the Lord Jesus Christ and in the Spirit of our God.

---

[15] Chapter X, Section 1.

I Corinthians 12:3: Therefore I want you to understand that no one speaking by the Spirit of God ever says "Jesus be cursed!" and no one can say "Jesus is Lord" except by the Holy Spirit.

II Corinthians 3:6: . . . the written code kills, but the Spirit gives life.

II Corinthians 3:17,18: Now the Lord is the Spirit, and where the Spirit of the Lord is, there is freedom. And we all, with unveiled face, beholding the glory of the Lord, are being changed into his likeness from one degree of glory to another; for this comes from the Lord who is the Spirit.

I Peter 1:2: . . . chosen and destined by God the Father and sanctified by the Spirit for obedience to Jesus Christ and for sprinkling with his blood . . .

B. Through regeneration or the new birth sinners are given spiritual life and made God's children. The Bible describes this process as a spiritual resurrection, a creation, the giving of a new heart, etc. The inward change, which is thus wrought through the Holy Spirit, results from God's power and grace, and in no way is He dependent upon man's help for success in this work.

1. Sinners, through regeneration, are brought into God's kingdom and are made His children. The *author* of this "second" birth is the Holy Spirit; the *instrument* which He uses is the word of God.

John 1:12,13: But to all who received him, who believed in his name, he gave power to become children of God; *who were born*, not of blood nor of the will of the flesh nor of the will of man, but *of God*.

John 3:3-8: Jesus answered him, "Truly, truly, I say to you, unless one is *born anew*, he cannot *see* the kingdom of God." Nicodemus said to him, "How can a man be born when he is old? Can he enter a second time into his mother's womb and be born?" Jesus answered, "Truly, truly, I say to you, unless one is born of water and the Spirit, he cannot *enter* the kingdom of God. That which is born of the flesh is flesh, and that which is *born of the Spirit* is spirit. Do not marvel that I said to you, 'You must be born anew.' The wind blows where it wills, and you hear the sound of it, but you do not know whence it comes or whither it goes; so it is with every one who is born of the Spirit."

Titus 3:5: . . . he saved us, not because of deeds done by us in righteousness, but in virtue of his own mercy, by the washing of *regeneration* and *renewal in the Holy Spirit*.

I Peter 1:3: Blessed be the God and Father of our Lord Jesus Christ! By his great mercy we have been *born anew* to a living hope through the resurrection of Jesus Christ from the dead.

I Peter 1:23: You have been *born anew*, not of perishable seed but of imperishable, through the living and abiding *word of God.*

I John 5:4: For whatever is *born of God* overcomes the world; and this is the victory that overcomes the world, our faith.

2. Through the Spirit's work the dead sinner is given a new heart (nature) and made to walk in God's law. In Christ he becomes a new creation.

Deuteronomy 30:6: And the Lord your God will *circumcise your heart* and the heart of your offspring, so that you will love the Lord your God with all your heart and with all your soul, that you may live.

Ezekiel 36:26,27: A *new heart* I will give you, and a *new spirit* I will put within you; and I will take out of your flesh the heart of stone and give you a heart of flesh. And I will put my spirit within you, and cause you to walk in my statutes and be careful to observe my ordinances. Compare Ezekiel 11:19.

Galatians 6:15: For neither circumcision counts for anything, nor uncircumcision, but *a new creation.*

Ephesians 2:10: For we are his workmanship, *created* in Christ Jesus for good works, which God prepared beforehand, that we should walk in them.

II Corinthians 5:17,18: Therefore, if any one is in Christ, he *is a new creation;* the old has passed away, behold, the new has come. All this is from God, who through Christ reconciled us to himself and gave us the ministry of reconciliation.

3. The Holy Spirit raises the sinner from his state of spiritual death and makes him alive.

John 5:21: For as the Father raises the dead and gives them life, so also the Son *gives life* to whom he will.

Ephesians 2:1,5: And you *he made alive,* when you were dead through the trespasses and sins . . . . even when we were dead through our trespasses, [God] made us *alive* together with Christ . . .

Colossians 2:13: And you, who were dead in trespasses and the uncircumcision of your flesh, *God made alive* together with him, having forgiven us all our trespasses.

C. God makes known to His chosen ones the secrets of the kingdom through the inward personal revelation given by the Spirit.

Matthew 11:25-27: At that time Jesus declared, "I thank thee, Father, Lord of heaven and earth, that thou hast hidden these things from the wise and understanding and revealed them to babes; yea, Father, for such was thy gracious will. All things have been delivered to me by my Father; and no one knows the Son except the Father, and no one *knows the Father* except the Son and any one to whom the Son *chooses to reveal him.*"

Luke 10:21: In that same hour he rejoiced in the Holy Spirit and said, "I thank thee, Father, Lord of heaven and earth, that thou hast hidden these things from the wise and 'understanding and *revealed* them to babes; yea, Father, for such was thy gracious will."

Matthew 13:10,11,16: Then the disciples came and said to him, "Why do you speak to them in parables?" And he answered them, "To you it has been *given to know the secrets* of the kingdom of heaven, but to them it has not been given .... But blessed are your eyes, for they *see,* and your ears, for they *hear.*"

Luke 8:10: "To you it has been *given to know* the secrets of the kingdom of God; but for others they are in parables, so that seeing they may not see, and hearing they may not understand."

Matthew 16:15-17: He said to them, "But who do you say that I am?" Simon Peter replied, "You are the Christ, the Son of the living God." And Jesus answered him, "Blessed are you, Simon Bar-Jona! For flesh and blood has not *revealed* this to you, but *my Father* who is in heaven."

John 6:37,44,45,64,65: "All that the Father *gives me will come to me;* and him who comes to me I will not cast out .... No one can come to me unless the Father who sent me *draws* him; and I will raise him up at the last day. It is written in the prophets, 'And they shall all be *taught* by God.' Every one who has *heard* and *learned from the Father* comes to me .... But there are some of you that do not believe." For Jesus knew from the first who those were that did not believe, and who it was that should betray him. And he said, "This is why I told you that no one can come to me unless it is *granted* him *by the Father.*"

I Corinthians 2:14: The unspiritual man does not receive the gifts of the Spirit of God, for they are folly to him, and he is not able to understand them because they are *spiritually discerned.*

Ephesians 1:17,18: ... that the God of our Lord Jesus Christ, the Father of glory, may *give* you a *spirit of wisdom and of revelation* in the knowledge of him, having *the eyes of your hearts enlightened,* that you may *know* what is the hope to which he has called you, ...

See also John 10:3-6, 16, 26-29.

D. *Faith* and *repentance* are *divine gifts* and are wrought in the soul through the regenerating work of the Holy Spirit.

Acts 5:31: "God exalted him at his right hand as Leader and Savior, to *give repentance* to Israel and forgiveness of sins."

Acts 11:18: When they heard this they were silenced. And they glorified God, saying, "Then to the Gentiles also God has *granted repentance* unto life."

Acts 13:48: And when the Gentiles heard this, they were glad and glorified the word of God; and as many as were *ordained* to eternal life *believed.*

Acts 16:14: One who heard us was a woman named Lydia, from the city of Thyatira, a seller of purple goods, who was a worshipper of God. *The Lord opened her heart* to *give heed* to what was said by Paul.

Acts 18:27: And when he wished to cross to Achaia, the brethren encouraged him, and wrote to the disciples to receive him. When he arrived, he greatly helped those who *through grace had believed.*

Ephesians 2:8,9: For by grace you have been saved through faith; and this is not your own doing, *it is the gift of God*—not because of works, lest any man should boast.

Philippians 1:29: For it has been *granted to you* that for the sake of Christ you should not only *believe* in him but also suffer for his sake.

II Timothy 2:25,26: ... God may perhaps *grant* that they will *repent* and come to *know* the truth, and they may escape from the snare of the devil, after being captured by him to do his will.

E. The gospel invitation extends a general outward call to salvation to all who hear the message. In addition to this external call, the Holy

Spirit extends a special inward call to the elect only. The general call of the gospel can be, and often is, rejected, but the special call of the Spirit cannot be rejected; it always results in the conversion of those to whom it is made.

Romans 1:6,7: . . . including yourselves who are *called* to belong to Jesus Christ; To all God's beloved in Rome, who are *called* to be saints . . .

Romans 8:30: And those whom he predestined he also *called;* and those whom he *called* he also justified; and those whom he justified he also glorified.

Romans 9:23,24: . . . in order to make known the riches of his glory for the vessels of mercy, which he has prepared beforehand for glory, even us whom he has *called*, not from the Jews only but also from the Gentiles?

I Corinthians 1:1,2,9,23-31: Paul, *called* by the will of God to be an apostle of Christ Jesus, and our brother Sosthenes, To the church of God which is at Corinth, to those sanctified in Christ Jesus, *called* to be saints . . . . God is faithful, by whom you were *called* into the fellowship of his Son, Jesus Christ our Lord . . . . but we preach Christ crucified, a stumbling block to Jews and folly to Gentiles, but to those who are *called*, both Jews and Greeks, Christ the power of God and the wisdom of God. For the foolishness of God is wiser than men, and the weakness of God is stronger than men.

For consider your *call*, brethren; not many of you were wise according to worldly standards, not many were powerful, not many were of noble birth; but God chose what is foolish in the world to shame the wise, God chose what is weak in the world to shame the strong, God chose what is low and despised in the world, even things that are not to bring to nothing things that are, so that no human being might boast in the presence of God. He is the source of your life in Christ Jesus, whom God made our wisdom, our righteousness and sanctification and redemption; therefore, as it is written, "Let him who boasts, boast of the Lord."

Galatians 1:15,16: But when he who had set me apart before I was born, and had *called* me through his grace, was pleased to reveal his Son to me, in order that I might preach him among the Gentiles, I did not confer with flesh and blood.

Ephesians 4:4: There is one body and one spirit, just as you were *called* to the one hope that belongs to your call.

II Timothy 1:9: ... who saved us and *called* us with a holy calling, not in virtue of our works but in virtue of his own purpose and the grace which he gave us in Christ Jesus ages ago.

Hebrews 9:15: Therefore he is the mediator of a new covenant, so that those who are *called* may receive the promised eternal inheritance ...

Jude 1: To those who are *called*, beloved in God the Father and kept for Jesus Christ.

I Peter 1:15: ... but as he who *called* you is holy, be holy yourselves in all your conduct.

I Peter 2:9: But you are a chosen race, a royal priesthood, a holy nation, God's own people, that you may declare the wonderful deeds of him who *called* you out of darkness into his marvelous light.

I Peter 5:10: And after you have suffered a little while, the God of all grace, who has *called* you to his eternal glory in Christ, will himself restore, establish, and strengthen you.

II Peter 1:3: His divine power has granted to us all things that pertain to life and godliness, through the knowledge of him who *called* us to his own glory and excellence.

Revelation 17:14: "... they will make war on the Lamb, and the Lamb will conquer them, for he is Lord of lords and King of kings, and those with him are *called* and chosen and faithful."

F. The application of salvation is all of grace and is accomplished solely through the almighty power of God.

Isaiah 55:11: " ... so shall my word be that goes forth from my mouth; it shall not return to me empty, but it shall *accomplish* that which *I purpose*, and prosper in the thing for which I sent it."

John 3:27: John answered, "No one can receive anything except what is *given* him from heaven."

John 17:2: " ... since thou hast given him power over all flesh, so that he might *give* eternal life to all whom thou hast given him."

Romans 9:16: So it depends not upon man's will or exertion, but upon *God's mercy.*

I Corinthians 3:6,7: I planted, Apollos watered, but *God gave the growth.* So neither he who plants nor he who waters is anything, but only God who *gives* the growth.

I Corinthians 4:7: For who sees anything different in you? What have you that you did not *receive?* If then you received it, why do you boast as if it were not a *gift?*

Philippians 2:12,13: Therefore, my beloved, as you have always obeyed, so now, not only as in my presence but much more in my absence, work out your own salvation with fear and trembling; for *God is at work in you,* both to *will* and to *work* for his good pleasure.

James 1:18: *Of his own will* he brought us forth by the word of truth that we should be a kind of first fruits of his creatures.

I John 5:20: And we know that the Son of God has come and has *given us understanding,* to *know* him who is true; and we are in him who is true, in his Son Jesus Christ. This is the true God and eternal life.

V. THE PERSEVERANCE OF THE SAINTS OR THE SECURITY OF BELIEVERS

The elect are not only redeemed by Christ and renewed by the Spirit; they are also *kept* in faith by the almighty power of God. All those who are spiritually united to Christ through regeneration are eternally secure in Him. Nothing can separate them from the eternal and unchangeable love of God. They have been predestined unto eternal glory and are therefore assured of heaven.

The doctrine of the perseverance of the saints does not maintain that all who *profess* the Christian faith are certain of heaven. It is *saints*—those who are set apart by the Spirit—who *persevere* to the end. It is *believers*—those who are given true, living faith in Christ— who are *secure* and safe in Him. Many who profess to believe fall away, but they do not fall from grace for they were never in grace. True believers do fall into temptations, and they do commit grievous sins, but these sins do not cause them to lose their salvation or separate them from Christ.

The Westminster Confession of Faith gives the following statement of this doctrine: "They whom God hath accepted in his Beloved, effectually called and sanctified by his Spirit, can neither totally nor finally fall away from the state of grace: but shall certainly persevere therein to the end, and be eternally saved."[16]

Boettner is certainly correct in asserting that "This doctrine does not stand alone but is a necessary part of the Calvinistic system of theology. The doctrines of Election and Efficacious Grace logically imply the certain salvation of those who receive these blessings. If God

---

[16] Chapter XIX, Section 1.

has chosen men absolutely and unconditionally to eternal life, and if His Spirit effectively applies to them the benefits of redemption, the inescapable conclusion is that these persons shall be saved."[17]

The following verses show that God's people are given *eternal life* the moment they believe. They are *kept by God's power* through faith and *nothing can separate them from His love*. They have been *sealed* with the Holy Spirit who has been given as the *guarantee* of their salvation, and they are thus assured of an eternal inheritance.

Isaiah 43:1-3: But now thus says the Lord, he who created you, O Jacob, he who formed you, O Israel: "Fear not, for I have redeemed you: I have called you by name, you are mine. When you pass through the waters I will be with you; and through the rivers, they shall not overwhelm you; when you walk through fire you shall not be burned, and the flame shall not consume you. For I am the Lord your God, the Holy One of Israel, your Savior."

Isaiah 54:10: "For the mountains may depart and the hills be removed, but my steadfast love shall not depart from you, and my covenant of peace shall not be removed, says the Lord, who has compassion on you."

Jeremiah 32:40: "I will make with them an everlasting covenant, that I will not turn away from doing good to them; and I will put the fear of me in their hearts, that they may not turn from me."

Matthew 18:12-14: "What do you think? If a man has a hundred sheep, and one of them has gone astray, does he not leave the ninety-nine on the hills and go in search of the one that went astray? And if he finds it, truly, I say to you, he rejoices over it more than over the ninety-nine that never went astray. So it is not the will of my Father who is in heaven that *one* of these little ones *should perish*."

John 3:16: For God so loved the world that he gave his only Son, that whoever believes in him *should not perish* but have *eternal life*.

John 3:36: He who believes in the Son *has eternal life* . . .

John 5:24: "Truly, truly, I say to you, he who hears my word and believes him who sent me *has eternal life;* he does *not come into judgment*, but *has passed from death to life*."

John 6:35-40: Jesus said to them, "I am the bread of life; he who comes to me shall *not hunger*, and he who believes in me shall *never thirst*. But I said to you that you have seen me and yet do not believe. All that the Father gives me will come to me; and *him who comes to me I will not cast out*. For I have come down from heaven, not to do my own will, but the will of him who sent me; and this is the will

---

[17] Boettner, *Predestination*, p. 182.

of him who sent me, that I should *lose nothing* of all that he has given me, but raise it up at the last day. For this is the will of my Father, that every one who sees the Son and believes in him should have eternal life; and I will raise him up at the last day."

John 6:47: "Truly, truly, I say to you, he who believes *has eternal life.*"

John 10:27-30: "My sheep hear my voice, and I know them, and they follow me; and I give them *eternal life,* and *they shall never perish,* and *no one shall snatch them out of my hand.* My Father, who has given them to me, is greater than all, and no one is able to snatch them out of the Father's hand. I and the Father are one."

John 17:11,12,15: "And now I am no more in the world, but they are in the world, and I am coming to thee. Holy Father, *keep them* in thy name which thou hast given me, that they may be one, even as we are one. While I was with them, I *kept them* in thy name which thou hast given me; I have guarded them, and *none of them is lost* but the son of perdition, that the scripture might be fulfilled . . . . I do not pray that thou shouldst take them out of the world, but that thou shouldst *keep them from the evil one.*"

Romans 5:8-10: But God shows his love for us in that while we were yet sinners Christ died for us. Since, therefore, we are *now justified* by his blood, *much more shall we be saved* by him *from the wrath of God.* For if while we were enemies we were reconciled to God by the death of his Son, much more, now that we are reconciled, shall we be *saved by his life.*

Romans 8:1: There is therefore now *no condemnation* for those who are in Christ Jesus.

Romans 8:29,30: For those whom he *foreknew* he also *predestined* to be conformed to the image of his Son, in order that he might be the first-born among many brethren. And those whom he predestined he also *called;* and those whom he called he also *justified;* and those whom he justified he also *glorified.*

Romans 8:35-39: Who shall separate us from the love of Christ? Shall tribulation, or distress, or persecution, or famine, or nakedness, or peril, or sword? As it is written, "For thy sake we are being killed all the day long; we are regarded as sheep to be slaughtered." No, in all these things we are *more than conquerors through him* who loved us. For I am sure that neither death, nor life, nor angels, nor principalities, nor things present, nor things to come, nor powers, nor height, nor depth, *nor anything else in all creation, will be able to separate us from the love of God in Christ Jesus our Lord.*

I Corinthians 1:7-9: . . . so that you are not lacking in any spiritual gift, as you wait for the revealing of our Lord Jesus Christ; who will *sustain you to the end, guiltless* in the day of our Lord Jesus Christ. *God is faithful,* by whom you were called into the fellowship of his Son, Jesus Christ our Lord.

I Corinthians 10:13: No temptation has overtaken you that is not common to man. God is faithful, and he will not let you be tempted *beyond your strength,* but with the temptation will also provide the way of escape, that you may be *able* to endure it.

II Corinthians 4:14,17: . . . knowing that he who raised the Lord Jesus will *raise us* also with Jesus and bring us with you into his presence . . . . For this slight momentary affliction is preparing us for an eternal weight of glory beyond all comparison.

Ephesians 1:5,13,14: He destined us in love to be his sons through Jesus Christ, according to the purpose of his will, . . . In him you also, who have heard the word of truth, the gospel of your salvation, and have believed in him, were *sealed* with the promised Holy Spirit, which is *the guarantee of our inheritance* until we acquire possession of it, to the praise of his glory.

Ephesians 4:30: And do not grieve the Holy Spirit of God, in whom you were *sealed* for the day of redemption.

Colossians 3:3,4: For you have died, and your life is hid with Christ in God. When Christ who is our life appears, then you also *will appear* with him *in glory.*

I Thessalonians 5:23,24: May the God of peace himself sanctify you wholly; and may your spirit and soul and body be *kept sound* and *blameless* at the coming of our Lord Jesus Christ. He who calls you is *faithful,* and *he will do it.*

II Timothy 4:18: The Lord will rescue me from every evil and save me for his heavenly kingdom. To him be the glory for ever and ever. Amen.

Hebrews 9:12,15: . . . he entered once for all into the Holy Place, taking not the blood of goats and calves but his own blood, thus *securing an eternal redemption* . . . . Therefore he is the mediator of a new covenant, so that those who are called may *receive* the *promised eternal inheritance,* since a death has occurred which redeems them from the transgressions under the first covenant.

Hebrews 10:14: For by a single offering he has *perfected for all time* those who are *sanctified.*

Hebrews 12:28: Therefore let us be grateful for *receiving* a kingdom that *cannot be shaken,* and thus let us offer to God acceptable worship, with reverence and awe.

I Peter 1:3-5: Blessed be the God and Father of our Lord Jesus Christ! By his great mercy *we have been born anew* to a living hope through the resurrection of Jesus Christ from the dead, and to an inheritance which is imperishable, undefiled, and unfading, kept in heaven for you, who by *God's power* are *guarded* through faith for a salvation ready to be revealed in the last time.

I John 2:19,25: They went out from us, but they were not of us; for if they had been of us, they would have *continued with us;* but they went out, that it might be plain that they all are not of us . . . . And this is what he has *promised us, eternal life.*

I John 5:4,11-13, 20: For whatever is born of God *overcomes* the world; and this is the victory that overcomes the world, our faith . . . . And this is the testimony, that *God gave us eternal life,* and this life is in his Son. He who has the Son *has life;* he who has not the Son has not life. I write this to you who believe in the name of the Son of God, that you may know that you *have eternal life* . . . . And we know that the Son of God has come and has given us understanding, to know him who is true; and we are in him who is true, in his Son Jesus Christ. This is the true God and eternal life.

Jude 1: To those who are called, beloved in God the Father and *kept* for Jesus Christ.

Jude 24,25: Now to him who is able to *keep you from falling* and to present you without blemish before the presence of his glory with rejoicing, to the only God, our Savior through Jesus Christ our Lord, be glory, majesty, dominion, and authority, before all time and now and for ever. Amen.

This brings to completion the second phase of our survey. We have by no means exhausted the Biblical texts which support the "five points." We hope, however, that enough evidence has been presented to show that these doctrines are drawn directly from the Holy Scriptures.

PART THREE

WORKS RECOMMENDED FOR THE STUDY OF CALVINISM

Introductory Remarks

In this, the third and final part of our survey, we shall briefly review a number of works that have been written in behalf of Calvinism. It is our hope that your interest has been stimulated and that you will make a serious study of this system of theology.

If you make such a study, you will find that "Calvinism is something much broader than the 'five points' indicate. Calvinism is a whole world-view, stemming from a clear vision of God as the whole world's Maker and King. Calvinism is the consistent endeavour to acknowledge the Creator as the Lord, working all things after the counsel of His will. Calvinism is a theocentric way of thinking about all life under the direction and control of God's own Word. Calvinism, in other words, is the theology of the Bible viewed from the perspective of the Bible—the God-centred outlook which sees the Creator as the source, and means, and end, of everything that is, both in nature and in grace. Calvinism is thus theism (belief in God as the ground of all things), religion (dependence on God as the giver of all things), and evangelicalism (trust in God through Christ for all things), all in their purest and most highly developed form. And Calvinism is a unified philosophy of history which sees the whole diversity of processes and events that take place in God's world as no more, and no less, than the outworking of His great pre-ordained plan for His creatures and His church. The five points assert no more than that God is sovereign in saving the individual, but Calvinism, as such, is concerned with the much broader assertion that He is sovereign everywhere." [18]

If, in your investigation, you probe into the history and influence of Calvinism, you will discover that its doctrines have been incorporated into the majority of the great creeds of the Protestant churches. For example, the Presbyterian and Reformed Churches, the Established Church of England and her daughter the Episcopal Church of America, the free church of Holland, almost all of the churches of Scotland, and in the main the Baptist and Congregationalist Churches both in England and America all possess creeds or confessions of faith which are Calvinistic in content.

Not only has Calvinism been incorporated into the creeds of the majority of the evangelical Protestant churches, it has also been championed by many of the churches' greatest theologians and preachers. A roll call of Calvinists would include such renowned leaders as Saint Augustine, John Wycliffe, Martin Luther, John Calvin, Ulrich Zwingli, Jerome Zanchius, Heinrich Bullinger, Martin Bucer, John Owen, George White-

---

[18] Packer, "Introductory Essay," (above, fn. 4), p. 5.

field, Augustus Toplady, John Bunyan, John Gill, John Newton, William Carey, Charles H. Spurgeon, Charles Hodge, William Cunningham, W. G. T. Shedd, A. H. Strong, B. B. Warfield, Abraham Kuyper, etc., etc.

The books and articles listed below (many of which are briefly introduced) will enable the reader to verify these claims for himself. These works set forth and defend, explain and clarify, state and answer objections to, and show the influence and value of Calvinistic theology.

The material is divided into two sections. SECTION ONE lists works which contain information relevant to the *overall Calvinistic system.* SECTION TWO lists works relating *specifically to each of the five points.* Since some of the books given in Section One contain important chapters or divisions that deal with the individual points, these works are repeated in Section Two, with the pertinent divisions and pages indicated. The first time a work is listed, we have given the author's full name, the title, the publisher's name and address, the date of publication, and the number of pages. Thereafter, only the author's last name and the title of the work are repeated. In many cases, explanatory remarks have been added to show the nature of the material covered in these books and its suitability for various classes of readers. Keep in mind that there are a number of *important books* discussed in Section Two under each of the five headings which *do not appear* in Section One.

Section One

WORKS DEALING WITH THE CALVINISTIC SYSTEM IN GENERAL OR WITH THE BROADER AREA OF GOD'S SOVEREIGNTY

I. BOOKS DEALING IN WHOLE OR IN PART WITH CALVINISM OR THE SOVEREIGNTY OF GOD

Boettner, Loraine. *The Reformed Doctrine of Predestination.* Philadelphia: Presbyterian and Reformed Publishing Co., 1963, 435 pages.

Of all the works on Calvinism with which we are familiar, this in our opinion is the best overall popular treatment of the subject. It is clear in style and logically arranged. Dr. Boettner has made good use of extensive quotations from a number of outstanding theological writers, both ancient and modern. These quotations not only serve to clarify the Calvinistic position but they also help to illustrate the fact that many of the leading Christian thinkers have endorsed and defended this system of thought. After giving a brief but good introduction to the issues under discussion, Boettner explains and defends at length each of the five points. He then states and answers objections commonly urged against Calvinism and closes with a survey of its influence upon history. We strongly recommend this work; it is one of those rare books written in a style that is readable and profitable for the beginner as well as for the more advanced student.

Bonar, Horatius, et/al. *The Five Points of Calvinism.* Jenkintown, Pa.: Sovereign Grace Publishers, n.d., 199 pages.

A collection of six articles written by Horatius Bonar, Andrew Fuller, John Calvin, John Gill, Thomas Goodwin, and Jonathan Edwards dealing with various aspects of Calvinism. These articles differ greatly in style and approach. To one seeking a unified survey of the five points or an introductory study of the system, this collection would not prove satisfactory. But for one who is interested in some solid discussions relating to these doctrines, the work will be helpful.

Booth, Abraham. *The Reign of Grace.* Grand Rapids: Wm. B. Eerdmans Publishing Co., 1949, 291 pages.

First published in England in 1768. The theme throughout is salvation by grace! Grace is shown to *reign* in the sinner's election, calling, justification, sanctification, etc. This is a sound and stimulating book.

Buis, Harry. *Historic Protestantism and Predestination.* Philadelphia: Presbyterian and Reformed Publishing Company, 1958, 142 pages.

A good concise history of the doctrine of predestination, written on a popular level. It identifies some of the leading opponents of predestination as well as many of its leading advocates. Buis goes to some length to establish the fact that Luther was a thoroughgoing predestinarian.

Calvin, John. *Calvin's Calvinism* (translated by Henry Beveridge). Grand Rapids: Wm. B. Eerdmans Publishing Co., 1950, 350 pages.

This book contains three treatises: The first is on the eternal predestination of God (pp. 25-186), the second is a brief reply (pp. 189-206) and the third deals with the secret providence of God (pp. 223-350). Calvin in a masterful way probes the depths of his subject. The material is not always easy reading, but it is extremely profitable. The great Reformer squarely faces the problems involved in these doctrines and constantly turns to the Scriptures for their solutions. This work will prove especially helpful in the study of the problem of evil.

Coles, Elisha. *A Practical Discourse of God's Sovereignty.* London: Thomas Tegg, 1845, 328 pages.

A 17th century work that has been republished many times but is out of print at the present. It consists of six practical discourses on God's Sovereignty, His Righteousness, Election, Redemption, Effectual Calling, and Perseverance. The edition given here (the forty-third) contains introductory recommendations from Thomas Goodwin (dated April 12, 1678), John Owen (not dated), and William Romaine (dated October 10, 1775). These alone indicate its excellence.

Copinger, Walter A. *A Treatise on Predestination, Election and Grace.* London: J. Nisbet, 1889, 465 pages.

This volume is not particularly notable for its treatment of the subject itself, although it may occasionally be perused with profit. The most significant feature of the work is undoubtedly the very extensive bibliography of the five points of Calvinism which is annexed to it; the bibliography is 235 pages of fine print. Here Copinger gives expression to his unusual talents as a bibliographer. He has undertaken to list all the works directly concerned with any of the five points of Calvinism, singly or in combination, from the time of the Apostles until the time of publication (1889). The entries are arranged chronologically and in the case of works which have appeared in several editions, a brief history of the printing is given. This bibliography is astonishingly complete and inclúdes many works of extreme rarity. Unfortunately, no work of comparable scope has been produced to bring this bibliography up to date. The specialists may find here a few errors and omissions. This book is unfortunately out of print and extremely scarce.

Cunningham, William. *Historical Theology.* London: The Banner of Truth Trust, 1960, 2 Vols., 1253 pages.

Cunningham was one of Scotland's greatest theologians. He served as Principal of New College, Edinburgh, from 1847 until his death in 1861. Charles Hodge regarded him as the foremost Reformed scholar of his day. *Historical Theology* is considered Cunningham's masterpiece. In Vol. II, he sets forth the historical development of Arminianism and Calvinism and shows the theological implication of each system. No serious student of theology can afford to neglect this important work.

Dickinson, Jonathan. *The True Scripture Doctrine.* Philadelphia: Presbyterian Board of Publication, n.d., 252 pages.

A valuable work which unfortunately is out of print. Dickinson limits his discussion to five discourses on Election, Original Sin, Conversion, Justification by Faith, and the Saint's Perseverance. The work is scholarly, logically arranged, and at the same time devotional. This latter feature is of particular worth, for Dickinson constantly appeals to the reader (especially in the summary of the chapters) to apply these doctrines to his life. This book deserves reprinting!

Edwards, John. *Veritas Redux.* London: Jonathan Robinson, etc., 1707, xxxviii, 558 pages.

This volume is a study of the five points of Calvinism by one of the great Puritan Calvinists of England. John Edwards (1637-1716) was thought to be one of the foremost Calvinists of his time, and this work represents the very mature presentation of his position both positively, by direct reference to Scriptural foundations, and negatively, by contrast with the Arminian point of view. The work is unfortunately out of print and very rare, but it is one of the plainest and most mature presentations of the Calvinistic point of view ever produced. Some publisher would do a great service to the cause of truth by reprinting this work.

Gill, John. *The Cause of God and Truth.* Atlanta, Ga.: Turner Lassetter, 1962, 328 pages.

In Part One Gill examines those passages most frequently appealed to by the Arminians in support of their system (60 texts are examined). Part Two is devoted to answering the arguments made by Arminians against passages which are appealed to by Calvinists in defense of their system. These texts are classified under the heads of the doctrines contained in the five points (62 passages are dealt with in this section). Part Three is a refutation of many of the standard arguments used by the Arminians in relation to the doctrines of reprobation, election, freedom of the will, the foreknowledge and providence of God, the state of the heathen, etc. Part Four deals with the testimony of the early Church fathers concerning these doctrines. Gill's exegesis and argumentation are outstanding.

Girardeau, John L. *Calvinism and Evangelical Arminianism: Compared As To Election, Reprobation, Justification, and Related Doctrines.* Columbia, S. C.: W. J. Duffie; and also New York: The Baker and Taylor Co., 1890, 574 pages.

The first 177 pages deal with Election and Reprobation. In this section Girardeau distinguishes Sublapsarianism from Supralapsarianism and insists that the former view is the position held by the main body of Calvinists. He then argues that Evangelical Arminianism has aimed much of its criticism at Calvinism *per se* instead of at Supralapsarian Calvinism. He claims that this has resulted in a lack of understanding of the Sublapsarian position and then attempts to show that the Sublapsarian (or Infralapsarian) view holds that the fall of Adam was avoidable and contingent and therefore not efficiently decreed by God. For our criticism of Girardeau's view of the fall, see our review of his work *The Will in Its Theological Relations,* p. 76. From p. 178 to p. 393 Girardeau answers objections to Calvinism based on the moral attributes of God, e.g., His Justice, Goodness, Wisdom, Veracity. Pages 394-412 deal with objections based on the moral agency of man. The remainder of the book (pp. 413-566) is devoted to the doctrine of justification. This volume contains much worthwhile material. The Presbyterian Reformation Society of Jackson, Mississippi, plans to reprint it soon.

Girod, Gordon. *The Deeper Faith.* Grand Rapids: Reformed Publications, 1958, 135 pages.

Written in a clear simple style; very easy to read. The first five chapters are based on the five Canons of Dort. Chapter six answers some of the objections that are commonly raised against these doctrines. Chapter seven is a reprint of the positive articles on the Five Points contained in these Canons. Boettner says of this work that it "is one of the clearest and most convincing statements of the distinguishing doctrines of the Reformed Faith that can be found anywhere."

Girod, Gordon. *The Way of Salvation.* Grand Rapids: Baker Book House, 1960, 175 pages.

Girod writes with great theological insight and homiletical skill. This work will prove very helpful to the pastor and layman alike.

Hayden, Eric W. *Spurgeon on Revival: A Biblical and Theological Approach.* Grand Rapids: Zondervan Publishing House, 1962, 144 pages.

In this work Hayden demonstrates the practical value of Calvinistic theology by showing the results it had in Spurgeon's ministry, especially during the great revival of 1859. In Ch. V, (pp. 85-138) entitled "What Spurgeon Preached During the Revival Year," the author documents the fact that Spurgeon not only held to, but vigorously proclaimed the five doctrines which make up the Calvinistic system. It is Hayden's contention that if we want a revival in our day then we should pattern our evangelism after Spurgeon's. Among other things, this would involve a return to these sound old doctrines. Cf. Spurgeon, *Sermons on Sovereignty,* below.

Kruithof, Bastian. *The High Points of Calvinism.* Grand Rapids: Baker Book House, 1949, 92 pages.

Composed of a series of eight sermons preached by the author to his congregation at the First Reformed Church of Holland, Michigan. The first chapter shows that the Calvinists do not hold to a "cold, theoretical, frosted religion," but rather that they earnestly desire to bear fruit for Christ. Chapter 2 is devoted to the Sovereignty of God, chapters 3-7 to the Five Points. The work ends with chapter 8 on "The Christian World and Life View." It is written on a popular level and will be helpful for the layman and new student.

Kuyper, Abraham. *Lectures on Calvinism.* Grand Rapids: Wm. B. Eerdmans Publishing Co., 1931, 298 pages.

This book consists of the six Stone Lectures which were delivered at Princeton Seminary in 1898, by the former Prime Minister of the

Netherlands. They begin with Calvinism as a Life-system (i.e., as a life and world view), then deal with Calvinism and Religion, Politics, Science, Art, and the Future. Kuyper was a theologian of the first order, as well as a statesman; these lectures reflect the keen powers of his mind.

McFetridge, N. S. *Calvinism in History.* Philadelphia: Presbyterian Board of Publication, 1882, 157 pages.

A good, short, simple treatment of Calvinism as a political, moral, and evangelizing force.

McNeill, John T. *The History and Character of Calvinism.* New York: Oxford University Press, 1954, 466 pages.

This volume has received warm recommendations from Calvinistic writers who, nevertheless, take sharp issue with its author's personal theological views. It is, for the greater part, fair, factual, and objective in its presentation of Calvinism and deserves serious attention. The work is divided into four sections. The first part deals with the Zwinglian background of the Genevan Reformation (pages 3-89). Part two is devoted to Calvin and the Reformation in Geneva (pages 93-234). Part three deals with the spread of Calvinism (pages 237-350). Part four discusses Calvinism and modern issues (pages 353-439). It is with this last section that most Calvinistic reviewers have taken issue; this part of the work should be read with critical discernment.

Packer, J. I. *Evangelism and the Sovereignty of God.* Chicago: Inter-Varsity Press, 1961, 126 pages; Paperback.

An excellent discussion of evangelism, its definition, its message, its motive, the methods and means by which it should be practiced, and its relation to the sovereignty of God in saving sinners. Packer shows that God's sovereignty and man's responsibility are taught side by side in the Bible; both are true and both must be believed and stressed if we are to do justice to the Biblical message. This book is of the highest quality; a much needed and penetrating treatment of the subject!

Packer, J. I. "Introductory Essay," John Owen, *The Death of Death in the Death of Christ.* London: The Banner of Truth Trust, 1959, pages 1-25.

This twenty-five page essay is a masterpiece in miniature. After briefly reviewing the origin and contents of the five points, Packer sets forth five reasons why Calvinism should not simply be equated with the "five points." In developing these five reasons, Packer makes some penetrating observations concerning the Calvinistic system as well as the Arminian system. By all means read this essay.

For our comments on the nature and value of Owen's work, which this essay introduces, see Point III below in Section Two of this bibliography.

Pink, Arthur W. *The Sovereignty of God.* London: The Banner of Truth Trust, 1961, 160 pages; Paperback.

This book deals with the sovereignty of God in creation, administration, salvation, and operation. Pink also develops the relationship between God's sovereignty and man's will, as well as its relation to prayer. He closes with a discussion of what our attitude should be toward this doctrine and its practical value in our lives. We have listed the revised British edition, rather than the American edition, for the following two reasons: first, its cost is considerably less since it is in a paperback and second, in our opinion, the deletions made in this revision have improved the work.

Rice, N. L. *God Sovereign and Man Free.* Cincinnati, Ohio: John D. Thorpe, 1850, 225 pages.

The book is divided into two sections: foreordination (pp. 9-115) and election (pp. 119-225). It makes a vigorous defense of both the sovereignty of God and the responsibility of man. A very good work, but as far as we know, it is out of print.

Smith, Egbert Watson. *The Creed of Presbyterians.* Richmond, Virginia: Presbyterian Committee of Publication, 1901, 223 pages.

A short textbook, written in a good style, on the history and doctrines of the Presbyterian Church, with a major section given to a study of the effects of Calvinism in the political and personal lives of its followers.

Smith, Morton H. *Studies in Southern Presbyterian Theology.* Jackson, Miss.: Presbyterian Reformation Society, 1962, 367 pages.

This volume first appeared as a doctoral dissertation under the direction of Professor G. C. Berkouwer. Its purpose is to trace the theological thought of some of the past leaders of the Southern Presbyterian Church, especially in relation to their views on the Inspiration of the Scriptures and the doctrine of Election. The author demonstrates the fact that the Southern Presbyterian Church of the past, at least, was under the capable leadership of men who were devoted to Calvinistic theology and the inerrancy of Scriptures. Among those discussed and whose theological works are briefly analyzed are Thornwell, Dabney, Palmer, Plumer, and Girardeau. The work contains an extensive bibliography on Southern Presbyterian theology.

Spurgeon, Charles Haddon. *Sermons on Sovereignty.* Ashland, Kentucky: Baptist Examiner Book Shop, 1959, 256 pages.

Spurgeon was probably the greatest Baptist preacher of all times. This volume contains a brief sketch of his life and a selection of eighteen sermons preached by him on various occasions in London, over a period of twenty-eight years. Each of these sermons deals with some aspect of Calvinism or of the Sovereignty of God. Such subjects as human inability, election, particular redemption, providence, etc., are covered. These messages were delivered to thousands who came to hear Spurgeon preach. See the review of *Spurgeon on Revival* by Hayden, above.

Warburton, Ben A. *Calvinism.* Grand Rapids: Wm. B. Eerdmans Publishing Co., 1955, 248 pages.

The full title of this book—*Calvinism: Its History and Basic Principles, Its Fruits and Its Future, and Its Practical Application to Life*—gives an outline of its contents. The book, written on a popular level, presents a good historical background of Arminius and the Synod of Dort. Among other things, the five articles of the Synod are explained and defended.

Warfield, Benjamin Breckinridge. *Calvin and Augustine.* Philadelphia: Presbyterian and Reformed Publishing Co., 1956, 507 pages.

This work consists of nine articles originally written for various theological journals and encyclopedias but later collected and published together. These studies are devoted to Calvin and Augustine and certain aspects of their thought. Directly or indirectly a good deal of the material is related to Calvinistic theology, although only one article is devoted to Calvinism itself. This work is a superb example of accurate scholarship, and the theological student will find the material exceedingly rich, although much of it will prove to be too technical for the average reader.

Warfield, Benjamin B. *The Plan of Salvation.* Grand Rapids: Wm. B. Eerdmans Publishing Co., 1955, 112 pages.

This small volume deals with the subject of "The Order of Decrees." There is an excellent chart on page 31 that summarizes the contents of the book. The vocabulary is heavy and at times the material is rather technical, which makes it somewhat difficult to read. But for those who are willing to study it, this is one of the most rewarding works ever written on the plan of salvation. Every student should make this a must on his reading list.

Zanchius, Jerome. *Absolute Predestination.* Jenkintown, Pa.: Sovereign Grace Publishers, n.d., 150 pages.

Written during the 16th century in Latin; translated into English by Augustus Toplady. The work consists of preliminary observations on the Divine Attributes and five chapters dealing with definitions of terms, predestination at large, election in particular, reprobation, and the duty of openly preaching these doctrines. It is regrettable that Toplady's preface has not been included in this edition. Due to its stiff style and formal argumentation, this book is difficult to read, but it will prove of value to the diligent student.

There are a number of important books (dealing specifically with each of the five points) discussed below in Section Two. For example, Edwards' *Freedom of the Will* and Luther's *Bondage of the Will* are listed and annotated under heading One entitled "Books Dealing with Human Inability and the Freedom of the Will."

II. ARTICLES IN REFERENCE WORKS OR SYSTEMATIC THEOLOGIES

All of the titles listed under this heading are standard works in the field of theology and should be given careful attention. These volumes contain articles or sections dealing with Calvinism or with the various Biblical doctrines related to the Calvinistic system. This material may be located in these works by consulting (1) the alphabetical arrangement of subjects, (2) the table of contents, or (3) the index, under such headings as the sovereignty of God, the decrees of God, Calvinism, original sin, depravity, election, predestination, atonement, satisfaction, grace, calling, regeneration, faith, perseverance, security of believers, etc.

It must not be supposed that because we have not commented upon the books contained in this section that they are of *less* value than the ones contained in the previous section. On the contrary, most of these works are so well known that they need no introduction, and, also, it would take an inordinate amount of space to describe their contents and to properly evaluate their importance. Therefore, we have refrained from commenting on any of them. *All of these works deserve serious study!*

Augustin, *The Nicene and Post-Nicene Fathers* (ed. by Philip Schaff), Vol. V. "Saint Augustine's Anti-Pelagian Works" with an introduction by B. B. Warfield. Grand Rapids: Wm. B. Eerdmans Publishing Co., 1956, 568 pages.

Baker's Dictionary of Theology (ed., Everett F. Harrison). Grand Rapids: Baker Book House, 1960, 566 pages.

Bavinck, Herman. *The Doctrine of God* (translated by William Hendriksen). Grand Rapids: Wm. B. Eerdmans Publishing Co., 1951, 407 pages.

Berkhof, L. *Systematic Theology.* Grand Rapids: Wm. B. Eerdmans Publishing Co., 1949, 784 pages.

Calvin, John. *Institutes of the Christian Religion. The Library of Christian Classics,* Vols. XX and XXI (ed. by John T. McNeill and tr. by F. L. Battles). Philadelphia: The Westminster Press, 1960.

Dabney, R. L. *Systematic and Polemic Theology*. Richmond, Va.: Presbyterian Committee of Publication, 1927, 903 pages.

Gill, John. *A Body of Doctrinal Divinity*. Grand Rapids: Baker Book House, n.d., 1023 pages.

Heppe, Heinrich. *Reformed Dogmatics, Set Out and Illustrated from the Sources* (translated by G. T. Thomson). London: George Allen and Unwin, 1950, 721 pages.

Hodge, Archibald Alexander. *Outlines of Theology*. Grand Rapids: Wm. B. Eerdmans Publishing Co., 1959, 678 pages.

Hodge, Charles. *Systematic Theology*. Grand Rapids: Wm. B. Eerdmans Publishing Co., 1952, 3 Vols.

Lecerf, Auguste. *An Introduction to Reformed Dogmatics*. London: Lutterworth Press, 1949.

Shedd, William G. T. *Dogmatic Theology*. Grand Rapids: Zondervan Publishing House, n.d., 3 Vols.

Strong, Augustus Hopkins. *Systematic Theology*. Chicago: The Judson Press, 1947, 1166 pages.

The New Bible Dictionary (ed., J. D. Douglas). Grand Rapids: Wm. B. Eerdmans Publishing Co., 1962, 1375 pages.

Warfield, Benjamin Breckinridge. *Biblical and Theological Studies*. Philadelphia: The Presbyterian and Reformed Publishing Co., 1952, 580 pages.

III. INFORMATION CONCERNING CREEDS AND CONFESSIONS OF FAITH

Below are listed the official confessions of faith of the majority of the major evangelical Protestant churches of the world. The fact that these confessions are Calvinistic in content testifies to the tremendous influence that Calvinism has exerted upon history. A number of other Calvinistic confessions could have been included, but it seemed best to confine the list to those confessions which have enjoyed an official capacity or (as in the case of the Baptists and the Congregationalists) have received the widest recognition among the churches. None of these confessions has been officially revised so as to exclude Calvinism, nor officially repudiated because of it. Of the Church of England, Lord Brougham said, "it has a Romish ritual, a Calvinistic creed, and an Arminian clergy." Since his time, more Protestant groups than wish to admit it have found themselves in the embarrassing position of possessing a Calvinistic confession and at the same time being dominated by ministers who believe and preach Arminianism while professing to be loyal to the historic doctrines of their churches.

For an excellent treatment of the study of the creeds, consult Philip Schaff's three volume work, *The Creeds of Christendom*, New York: Harper and Brothers, 1919. Volume I gives a history of the creeds, Volume II is devoted to the Greek and Latin Creeds, and Volume III contains the texts of all the major evangelical creeds. See also the recent book by W. L. Lumpkin, *Baptist Confessions of Faith*, Chicago: The Judson Press, 1959, 430 pages. This work contains a brief historical sketch of the Baptist movement along with all of its major confessions given in full.

The other books given in this section are devoted to the study of the particular creeds under which they appear.

The Major Confessions of the Reformed or Calvinistic Churches

A. The Second Helvetic Confession, A.D. 1564 (Thirty Chapters). For the sections relating to Calvinistic doctrines, see Chs. VI, VII, IX, X, XIV, and XVI.

   This confession was adopted by the Reformed Churches in Switzerland, Poland, Hungary, Scotland, and France.

B. The Thirty-nine Articles of the Church of England, A.D. 1562. See Articles IX, X, XI, and XVII.

   These articles constitute the doctrinal standard of the Episcopal Churches in England, Scotland, America and the Commonwealth Nations. The Episcopal Church of America made some slight alterations, but these did not affect the Calvinistic element of the thirty-nine articles.

C. The Belgic Confession, A.D. 1561 (Thirty-seven Articles). See Articles XIII, XIV, XV, XXI, XXII, and XXIII.

   This confession, along with the positive articles of the Canons of Dort and the Heidelberg Catechism, forms the official standard of the French and Dutch Reformed Churches as well as the Reformed Church of America.

   Ursinus, Zacharias. *Commentary on the Heidelberg Catechism.* Grand Rapids: Wm. B. Eerdmans Publishing Co., 1954, 659 pages.

D. The Canons of the Synod of Dort, A.D. 1619. See all five chapters. The positive articles are given in Gordon Girod's book, *The Deeper Faith.*

E. The Westminster Confession, A.D. 1646 (Thirty-three Chapters). See Chapters III, V, VI, VII, IX, X, XIV, XV, and XVII.

   This, the most famous of all the Reformed Confessions, along with the Larger and Shorter Catechisms, forms the common doctrinal standard of all Presbyterian Churches of English and Scotch derivation. A. A. Hodge observes that "It is also of all Creeds the one most highly approved by all the bodies of Congregationalists in England and America." Over sixty leading scholars met in 1,163 sessions during a five and one-half year period in order to draw up this Confession along with the two Catechisms. The following commentaries on this great Confession will be of real value in its study.

Clark, Gordon H. *What Presbyterians Believe.* Philadelphia: Presbyterian and Reformed Publishing Co., 1956, 130 pages.

> This is a fine exposition of the Westminster Confession written by a contemporary scholar. Dr. Clark is not only a brilliant student in the field of theology and philosophy, but is also an unusually gifted writer who has the rare talent of making his subject clear and interesting. This work is written on a popular level; do not fail to read it.

Green, J. B. *A Harmony of the Westminster Standards.* Richmond, Virginia: John Knox Press, 1951, 231 pages.

Hodge, A. A. *The Confession of Faith.* London: Banner of Truth Trust, 1958, 430 pages.

> Professor F. L. Patton of Princeton Seminary said of it, "This book provides probably the finest concise exposition of the greatest systematic Confession of Faith in the English Language." Hodge, here as elsewhere, demonstrates his ability as a thinker and writer. By all means consult this book.

F. The Savoy Declaration, A.D. 1658 (Thirty-two Chapters). See Chapters III, V, VI, VII, IX, X, XIV, XV, and XVII.

> Schaff says of the creeds or declarations of faith which have been approved by the Congregational Churches in England and America that "They agree substantially with the Westminster Confession, or the Calvinistic system of doctrine, but differ from Presbyterianism by rejecting the legislative and judicial authority of presbyteries and synods, and by maintaining the independence of the local churches" (Vol. I, p. 829). Of all the Congregational creeds, the Savoy Declaration of 1658 is perhaps the most important. Schaff observes that it "is the work of a committee, consisting of Drs. Goodwin, Owen, Nye, Bridge, Caryl, and Greenhill, who had been members of the Westminster Assembly, with the exception of Dr. Owen. It contains a lengthy Preface (fourteen pages), the Westminster Confession of Faith with sundry changes (twenty-two pages), and a Platform of Church Polity (five pages)" (Vol. I, p. 832).

Because of the close identity between the Savoy Declaration and the Westminster Confession, the commentaries listed above, under the latter, will serve as excellent guides in the study of this Declaration.

G. The (Second) London Confession, A.D. 1688 (Thirty-two Chapters). See Chapters III, V, VI, VII, IX, X, XIV, XV, and XVII.

This historic English Baptist Confession (drawn up in 1677) was adopted in America by the Philadelphia Baptist Association in 1742 with two articles added, bringing the number of chapters to thirty-four and causing the renumbering of Chapters XXIII to XXXIV. In this country, it has ever since been known as the "Philadelphia Confession." It is, as Schaff observes, "simply the Baptist recension of the Westminster Confession, . . . with very few verbal alterations, except in the doctrine of the Church and the Sacraments" (Vol. I, p. 885). The Baptists gave two reasons for following the Westminster Confession so closely: first, they wanted to emphasize the agreement between the two groups, and second, they had "no itch to clog religion with new words . . . ." This Confession has exerted greater influence and received wider recognition among the Baptists of England and America than any other statement of doctrine.

Because of the close identity between the two, the commentaries listed above on the Westminster Confession will also serve as excellent guides in the study of this Confession. A recent edition of the London Confession (32 Articles) has been published in this country by Jay Green under the title, *The Philadelphia Confession of Faith*, Jenkintown, Pa.: Sovereign Grace Publishers, n.d., 144 pages.

IV. BOOKLETS, PAMPHLETS, OR TRACTS

The names and addresses of the following publishers are given (along with selected titles of tracts and pamphlets handled by them) for the benefit of those who are interested in obtaining or distributing Calvinistic literature in this form. Information concerning prices and other titles can be obtained from these publishers upon request.

A. Baker Book House
    Grand Rapids, Michigan

    Gerstner, John H. "A Predestination Primer." 51 pages.

B. Bible Truth Depot
    Swengel (Union County), Pennsylvania

    Cole, C. D. "The Bible Doctrine of Election." 23 pages.

    Fletcher, George B. "Predestination." 22 pages.

Harbach, Rev. Robert C. "Calvinism . . . The Truth." 15 pages.

Ness, Christopher. "An Antidote Against Arminianism." 110 pages.

Pink, Arthur W. "The Atonement." 28 pages.

Pink, Arthur W. "The Attributes of God." 83 pages.

Pink, Arthur W. "The Doctrine of Election." 32 pages.

Pink, Arthur W. "The Godhead of God." 31 pages.

Pink, Arthur W. "The Holy Spirit's Work in Salvation." 16 pages.

Pink, Arthur W. "The New Birth." 32 pages.

Pink, Arthur W. "Sins of the Saints—Including Preservation and Perseverance." 37 pages.

Spurgeon, C. H. "A Defence of Calvinism." 19 pages.

Spurgeon, C. H. "Election." 23 pages.

C. Committee on Christian Education
Orthodox Presbyterian Church
728 Schaff Building, 1505 Race Street
Philadelphia, Pennsylvania

Hamilton, Floyd E. "The Reformed Faith in the Modern World." 32 pages.

Murray, John. "The Sovereignty of God." 32 pages.

Murray, John and Ned B. Stonehouse. "The Free Offer of the Gospel." 27 pages.

D. Moelker Printing Company
Grand Rapids, Michigan

Palmer, Edwin H. "The Five Points of Calvinism." 88 pages.

E. Presbyterian Reformation Society
P.O. Box 1501
Jackson, Mississippi

Reed, R. C. "The Gospel As Taught By Calvin." 157 pages.

Section Two

SELECTED REFERENCES RELATING TO EACH OF THE FIVE POINTS INDIVIDUALLY

Some of the books listed above in Section One under heading I, which contain chapters or divisions that deal significantly with the individual points of Calvinism, are repeated in this section of the bibliography with the appropriate divisions and pages indicated. Because of the lack of space, we had to refrain from referring to the materials contained in the reference works, systematic theologies, creeds and booklets, listed under headings II, III, and IV of Section One. Those works listed under heading II, although *not* repeated here, should be given *special attention* in the study of *each* of the five points.

I. BOOKS DEALING WITH HUMAN INABILITY AND THE FREE-DOM OF THE WILL

Boettner. *The Reformed Doctrine of Predestination.* Ch. X, (pp. 61-82).

Boston, Thomas. *Human Nature in its Fourfold State.* Jenkintown, Pa.: Sovereign Grace Publishers, 1957, 360 pages.

First published in 1720 and republished many times since. This is written in the style of the Puritans and is not an easy book to read, but it contains some worthwhile material. Pages 23-92 deal with human depravity and pages 118-130 with human inability.

Clark, Gordon H. *Religion, Reason and Revelation.* Philadelphia: Presbyterian and Reformed Publishing Co., 1961, 241 pages.

Part V of this book deals with the problem of "God and Evil" (pp. 194-241). There is an excellent discussion of "free-will" throughout this section. Clark's logic and arguments are devastating to the Arminian position.

Cunningham. *Historical Theology.* Vol. I, pp. 333-346 and pp. 496-639.

Edwards, Jonathan. *Freedom of the Will* (edited by Paul Ramsey). New Haven, Connecticut: Yale University Press, 1957, 494 pages.

A classic! Ramsey says of it, "This book alone is sufficient to establish its author as the greatest philosopher-theologian yet to grace the American scene." Edwards' purpose is to show that the Arminian view of the freedom of the will is both unreasonable and unscriptural. To quote Ramsey, "Edwards' argument in this treatise rests upon two pillars: the proof from biblical revelation and the proof from reason." Although first published in 1754, the arguments set forth in this work have never been answered by the Arminians. It requires hard study, but no serious student can afford to neglect it.

Gill. *The Cause of God and Truth.* Part II, Ch. V, (pp. 122-130) and Part III, Ch. V, (pp. 183-198).

Girardeau, John L. *The Will in Its Theological Relations.* Columbia, S. C.: W. J. Duffie; and also New York: The Baker and Taylor Co., 1891, 497 pages.

This is a heavy technical effort to explain the nature of the freedom of the will. The màjor part of the work centers around the freedom of Adam's will before the fall. The author contends that Edwards and Calvin did not hold identical views with regard to the nature of the liberty of will and he makes a fair case for saying that he is in agreement with Calvin on this matter. However, after establishing this point, Girardeau then argues that the fall was avoidable and contingent and not efficiently decreed by God. Here he admits that he must disagree with Calvin who taught the freedom of Adam's will but at the same time held that Adam's fall was decreed and therefore unavoidable. In insisting on the avoidability of the fall Girardeau parts company with mainline Calvinism. We feel that his arguments in support of this position are based on philosophical speculation rather than Biblical evidence. The work is presently out of print.

Girod. *The Deeper Faith.* Ch. III, (pp. 46-60).

Luther, Martin. *The Bondage of the Will* (tr. by J. I. Packer and O. R. Johnston). Westwood, New Jersey: Fleming H. Revell Co., 1957, 320 pages.

Luther considered this his most significant contribution to the study of theology. As the translators of this edition state, it is "one of the enduring monuments of evangelical doctrine; a masterpiece in the realm of polemics, dogmatics and exegesis." Warfield said of it, "it is . . . in a true sense the manifesto of the Reformation." This new translation by Packer and Johnston with its forty-eight page "Historical and Theological Introduction," greatly enhances its value. As the translators state, "It was man's total inability to save himself, and the sovereignty of Divine grace in his salvation, that Luther was affirming when he denied 'free-will' . . . . The deepest truth about him [fallen man] is that his *arbitrium*, his power and exercise of choice, is *enslaved*—to sin and Satan; and his natural condition is one of total inability to merit anything other than wrath and damnation" (pp. 48, 50, 51). This is one of the great classics of Calvinistic literature and merits serious study.

Spurgeon. *Sermons on Sovereignty.* pp. 121-133, text John 6:44.

Warburton. *Calvinism.* Ch. 7, (pp. 126-148).

Consult the works listed in Section One under heading II.

II. BOOKS DEALING WITH ELECTION AND PREDESTINATION

Berkouwer, G. C. *Divine Election* (tr. by Hugo Bekker). Grand Rapids: Wm. B. Eerdmans Publishing Co., 1960, 336 pages.

A recent and important contribution to this field of study, written by one of the foremost theologians of our day. The theological student should not neglect this monumental work; it reflects the wide reading and penetrating thought of its author, who is Professor of Systematic

Theology at the Free University in Amsterdam. This is the seventh volume of Berkouwer's series "Studies in Dogmatics." For some pertinent observations concerning this work see Gordon H. Clark's remarks in *Religion, Reason and Revelation*, pp. 233 ff.

Boettner. *The Reformed Doctrine of Predestination.* Ch. XI, (pp. 83-149).

Booth. *The Reign of Grace.* Ch. III, (pp. 53-97).

Coles. *A Practical Discourse of God's Sovereignty.* pp. 54-120.

Cunningham. *Historical Theology.* Vol. II, pp. 416-490.

Gill. *The Cause of God and Truth.* Part II, Ch. 1, (pp. 71-78) Ch. 2, (pp. 78-94) and Part III, Ch. 1, (pp. 149-158) Ch. 2, (pp. 158-168).

Girod. *The Deeper Faith.* Ch. I, (pp. 13-28).

Klooster, Fred. *Calvin's Doctrine of Predestination.* Grand Rapids: Calvin Theological Seminary, 1961, 77 pages.

In this study Dr. Klooster gives an excellent analysis of Calvin's doctrine of "double" predestination. He carefully documents the fact that Calvin held to the equal ultimacy of both election and reprobation. This monograph deserves the attention of all who desire to understand the great Reformer's position as well as those who wish to sharpen their own thinking in this area. Besides being well documented it contains a helpful bibliography.

Murray, John. *Calvin on Scripture and Divine Sovereignty.* Grand Rapids: Baker Book House, 1960, 71 pages.

This small volume contains three lectures, the last of which (16 pages in length) is devoted to Calvin's doctrine of God's sovereignty in election and reprobation as well as in His providential control of all events both good and evil. A superb treatment of the subject and well documented.

Rice. *God Sovereign and Man Free.* Part II, (pp. 119-225).

Spurgeon. *Sermons on Sovereignty.* pp. 51-67, text II Thess. 2:13,14; pp. 69-93, text I Thess. 1:4-6.

Thornwell, James H. *Election and Reprobation.* Jackson, Mississippi: Presbyterian Reformation Society, 1961, 97 pages; Paperback. Also published in paperback by The Presbyterian and Reformed Publishing Co., Philadelphia, Pa.

The author begins by giving a clear statement of the doctrines of Election and Reprobation as set forth in the Standards of the Presbyterian Church (pp. 5-8). He then shows that these doctrines are vindicated by the Word of God (pp. 8-44). In pages 44-87 various objections are dealt with. Thornwell closes by drawing some inferences from these doctrines (pp. 87-97). This work (which was written in 1840) is characterized by clarity, directness, and what is more important, sound Biblical exegesis. It is regrettable that a table of contents and an index of the Biblical texts dealt with were not included in this reprint. We highly recommend this work.

Warburton. *Calvinism.* Ch. 5, (pp. 80-106).

Consult the works listed in Section One under heading II.

III. BOOKS DEALING WITH THE NATURE AND EXTENT OF THE ATONEMENT

One should not attempt to settle the question of the *extent* or *intended application* of Christ's atoning work until he first considers the broader question of the *nature* or *purpose* of the atonement. Before asking the profound question *"for whom* did Christ die?" one should first ask the more fundamental question, *"why* did Christ die?" Or to state it more pointedly, *"what* was *accomplished* by His death?" The works by Crawford, Hodge, and the two volumes by Smeaton, listed below, are especially recommended for the overall study of Christ's redeeming work. Owen's book will prove to be of particular value to those who will devote the time and effort required to read it.

Berkhof, Louis. *Vicarious Atonement Through Christ.* Grand Rapids: Wm. B. Eerdmans Publishing Co., 1936, 184 pages.

A brief survey of the doctrine of Christ's substitutionary atonement. Well written and easy to read. The last two sections (pp. 151-178) deal with the restricted design of the atonement.

Boettner. *The Reformed Doctrine of Predestination.* Ch. XII, (pp. 150-161).

Coles. *A Practical Discourse of God's Sovereignty.* pp. 120-192.

Crawford, Thomas J. *The Doctrine of the Holy Scriptures Respecting the Atonement.* Grand Rapids: Baker Book House, 1954, 538 pages.

Crawford first sets forth the doctrine of the New Testament respecting the Atonement (pp. 3-202). He then confirms the New Testament doctrine by appealing to the teaching contained in the Old Testament (pp. 203-284). Next he reviews the various theories respecting the suffering of Christ which have been substituted for the Biblical doctrine (pp. 284-401), as well as the objections which have been made against the Scriptural doctrine (pp. 403-489). This is an excellent work, well outlined and thoroughly indexed. Every student's library should include this volume. On the definite design of Christ's saving work, see pp. 122, 148-157, 196-202, and Note G, pp. 510-516.

PART III: THE FIVE POINTS DOCUMENTED

Cunningham. *Historical Theology*. Vol. II, pp. 237-370.

Gill. *The Cause of God and Truth*. Part II, Ch. III, (pp. 98-104) and Part III, Ch. III, (pp. 163-178).

Girod. *The Deeper Faith*. Ch. II (pp. 29-45).

Hodge, Archibald Alexander. *The Atonement*. Grand Rapids: Wm. B. Eerdmans Publishing Co., 1953, 440 pages.

Whereas Crawford's work, listed above, and Smeaton's two volumes, given below, use the "inductive" method in the study of the atonement, Hodge chose the "dogmatic" approach. His work is divided into two parts. Part I deals with the *Nature* of the Atonement (pp. 13-346). In this section Hodge carefully defines the doctrine and the major terms to be used in its study, after which he sets out to systematically establish it upon Biblical grounds. Part II is devoted to the *Design* or *Intended Application* of the Atonement (pp. 347-429). This section contains a superb explanation and defense of the doctrine of limited atonement. By all means study this work!

Kuiper, R. B. *For Whom Did Christ Die?* Grand Rapids: Wm. B. Eerdmans Publishing Co., 1959, 104 pages.

This book is concerned with "A Study of the Divine Design of the Atonement." It deals with the unscriptural views of the atonement under the heads of Unrestricted Universalism, Arminian Universalism, and Barthian Universalism. The Scriptural view is divided into two sections, Scriptural Particularism and Scriptural Universalism. The former deals with "special grace" and the latter with "common grace." A good work which deserves attention.

Murray, John. *Redemption—Accomplished and Applied*. Grand Rapids: Wm. B. Eerdmans Publishing Co., 1955, 236 pages. Available also in paperback.

Part One deals with the necessity, nature, perfection, and extent of the atonement, and Part Two discusses its application through effectual calling, regeneration, faith and repentance, justification, etc. A very fine treatment of the subject.

Owen, John. *The Death of Death in the Death of Christ*. London: The Banner of Truth Trust, 1959, 312 pages.

In the opening words of the "Introductory Essay" Packer states that this "is a polemic work, designed to show, among other things, that the doctrine of universal redemption is unscriptural and destructive of the gospel." It was first published in 1648. The work is divided into four books. Books I and II contain a survey of the Biblical account of redemption arranged with a view of determining its intended and accomplished end. Book III contains sixteen arguments against the "general ransom" idea. Book IV contains a refutation of the exegetical and theological arguments for universal redemption which Owen had encountered. This is one of the most thorough defenses of the doctrine of limited atonement ever written. Packer's analysis of Owen's work (pp. 26-31) will prove to be of untold value in its study. His introduction to this new edition is worth the price of the book. See our comments in Section One, under heading I, concerning Packer's "Introductory Essay."

Pink, Arthur W. *The Satisfaction of Christ.* Swengel, Pennsylvania: Bible Truth Depot, 1955, 313 pages.

Twenty-four chapters dealing with the doctrine of the Atonement written on a popular level. Chapters 19 and 20 (pp. 240-265) discuss the extent of the atonement. We cannot always agree with Pink's exegesis (e.g., he is given to excessive typology and at times he rests arguments upon texts that are improperly translated or are out of context) but in spite of these occasional flaws, his writings contain much that is sound and edifying.

Smeaton, George. *The Apostles' Doctrine of the Atonement.* Grand Rapids: Zondervan Publishing House, 1957, 548 pages.

In this work Smeaton expounds the doctrine of the Atonement by appealing to the teachings of the apostles. In the work which immediately follows he treats the same subject but bases his exegesis on the *teachings* of *Christ.* The two volumes together deal with all of the significant passages in the New Testament relating to the doctrine of the Atonement. Both works are well outlined and well indexed. At the end of the volume on the Apostles' doctrine, there is a sixty-six page historical sketch of the doctrine, which explains the views of the atonement held by such men as Augustine, Calvin, Arminius, Amyraldus, etc. Wilbur Smith says of Smeaton that he "was in his day considered the outstanding Calvinistic theologian of Scotland . . . ." These two volumes will prove an invaluable aid in the study of this important subject. Do not neglect them.

Smeaton, George. *The Doctrine of the Atonement as Taught by Christ Himself.* Grand Rapids: Zondervan Publishing House, 1953, 502 pages.

See comments under the above title, *The Apostles' Doctrine of the Atonement.*

Spurgeon. *Sermons on Sovereignty.* pp. 81-93, text Matt. 20:28; pp. 95-105, text Psa. 130:9.

Warburton. *Calvinism.* Ch. 6, (pp. 107-125).

Consult the works listed in Section One under heading II.

IV. BOOKS DEALING WITH EFFICACIOUS GRACE

Since the doctrine of Efficacious Grace is so vitally connected with the doctrine of the Holy Spirit and His work, we suggest that they be studied in conjunction with one another. The books below, by Owen, Kuyper, Smeaton, and Winslow, will prove invaluable in the study of the overall work of the Spirit as well as in the study of His special work of effectually drawing the elect to Christ.

Boettner. *The Reformed Doctrine of Predestination.* Ch. XIII, (pp. 162-181).

Coles. *A Practical Discourse of God's Sovereignty.* pp. 193-259.

Cunningham. *Historical Theology.* Vol. I, pp. 346-355; Vol. II, pp. 394-416.

Gill. *The Cause of God and Truth.* Part II, Ch. IV, (pp. 105-121) Part III, Ch. IV, (pp. 178-183).

Girod. *The Deeper Faith.* Ch. IV, (pp. 61-75).

Kuiper, Herman. *By Grace Alone.* Grand Rapids: Wm. B. Eerdmans Publishing Co., 1955, 165 pages.

> A study of "The Ordo Salutis" (the order of salvation). It deals with the application of Christ's redeeming work to sinners. Such subjects as Calling, Regeneration, Faith and Conversion, Justification, Sanctification, Preservation, and Glorification are admirably covered. It is well written, and very logically arranged, but somewhat technical at points. This is a good treatment of an important subject.

Kuyper, Abraham. *The Work of the Holy Spirit.* Grand Rapids: Wm. B. Eerdmans Publishing Co., 1941, 664 pages.

> This work consists of three volumes in one. The first volume deals with the work of the Holy Spirit in the Church as a whole; the second and third volumes are devoted to the Holy Spirit's work in the individual. Warfield said of this book, "it brings together the material belonging to this great topic with a systematizing genius that is very rare, . . ." There is no doubt that this is one of the most important studies ever written on this profound subject. In relation to the doctrine of Efficacious Grace note especially the material contained in Vol. II, pp. 203-427.

Murray. *Redemption—Accomplished and Applied.* Part II, Chs. 1-4, (pp. 97-143).

Owen, John. *The Holy Spirit, His Gifts and Power* (edited by George Buirder). Grand Rapids: Kregel Publications, 1954, 356 pages.

This classic work on the Holy Spirit covers such topics as His name, nature, personality, dispensations, operations, and effects. John Owen was probably the most renowned of all the Puritan writers, and this is considered by some to be his masterpiece. For over 250 years, it has received the highest recognition. Abraham Kuyper, who himself produced a monumental work on this subject, said of Owen's work that it is the "most widely known and still unsurpassed." The half century that has elapsed since Kuyper made this evaluation has not altered the situation. In connection with the doctrine of Efficacious Grace see Book III, pp. 119-218.

Palmer, Edwin H. *The Holy Spirit.* Grand Rapids: Baker Book House, 1958, 174 pages.

This book will prove especially helpful for those who are just beginning a study of the Holy Spirit and His work. It is written in a clear, simple style and is well outlined. In connection with the efficacious work of the Spirit, see Ch. 3 (pp. 29-39), Ch. 5 (pp. 53-61), Ch. 7 (pp. 77-86), and Ch. 14 (pp. 165-174).

Smeaton, George. *The Doctrine of the Holy Spirit.* London: The Banner of Truth Trust, 1958, 372 pages.

We have had occasion already to refer to Smeaton's reputation as a theologian and scholar (under Point III). This work on the Holy Spirit is of the same high quality as his two volumes on the Atonement. Dr. Caspar W. Hodge of Princeton recommended Smeaton's book on the Holy Spirit as the best on the subject. Lecture IV entitled "The Spirit's Regenerating Work on the Individual" (pp. 162-203) deals with the subject of Efficacious Grace. At the end of the book Smeaton gives an excellent "Historical Survey of the Doctrine of the Holy Spirit from the Apostolic Age" (pp. 256-368). Pages 291-368 are devoted to the history of the work of the Spirit; they give a survey of the different positions held by the major theologians and confessions of faith in relation to the efficacious call of the Spirit, as well as a brief review of many of the books written on the subject prior to 1882. By all means consult this work!

Spurgeon. *Sermons on Sovereignty.* pp. 135-146, text Gen. 12:5.

Warburton. *Calvinism.* Ch. 8, (pp. 149-168).

Winslow, Octavius. *The Work of the Holy Spirit.* London: The Banner of Truth Trust, 1961, 223 pages; Paperback.

The author exhibits a clear insight into the work of the Holy Spirit as well as a deep regard for the person of the Spirit as a member of the Godhead. The work is fairly comprehensive without being technical. Chapters two and three, entitled "The Spirit a Quickener," (pp. 31-86) discuss the Spirit's work with regard to Efficacious Grace. First published in 1843.

Consult the works listed in Section One under heading II.

V. BOOKS DEALING WITH THE PERSEVERANCE OF THE SAINTS

Berkouwer, G. C. *Faith and Perseverance* (tr. by Robert D. Knudsen). Grand Rapids: Wm. B. Eerdmans Publishing Co., 1958, 256 pages.

A very penetrating treatment of the doctrine of the Perseverance of the Saints and of its place in the history of the Church. This doctrine is examined against the backdrop of the Reformed Standards (in Ch. 2) and the three major controversies which have arisen over the subject of Perseverance (in Ch. 3)—namely the controversies between the Reformed or Calvinistic theologians and (1) the Remonstrants (the Arminian party of Holland), (2) the Roman Catholics and (3) the Lutherans. The problem of Perseverance as it relates to Admonition, Prayer, and Temptation is discussed in Chs. 4, 5, and 6, respectively. Berkouwer concludes in Chs. 7 and 8 by showing the Consolation and Reality of Perseverance. This valuable contribution throws much light on this blessed doctrine. Although the book may be difficult in places for the beginning student, the effort spent reading it will not be misused.

Boettner. *The Reformed Doctrine of Predestination.* Ch. XIV, (pp. 182-200).

Coles. *A Practical Discourse of God's Sovereignty.* pp. 259-328.

Cunningham. *Historical Theology.* Vol. I, pp. 355-358; Vol. II, pp. 490-501.

Gill. *The Cause of God and Truth.* Part II, Ch. VI, (pp. 131-149); Part III, Ch. VI, (pp. 198-202).

Girod. *The Deeper Faith.* Ch. V, (pp. 76-90).

Kuiper. *By Grace Alone.* Ch. VII, (pp. 138-147).

Murray. *Redemption—Accomplished and Applied.* Part II, Ch. 8, (pp. 189-198).

Spurgeon. *Sermons on Sovereignty.* pp. 201-214, text Job 17:9.

Warburton. *Calvinism.* Ch. 9, (pp. 169-188).

Consult the works listed in Section One under heading II.

* * * * *

May God grant each of us the desire to *study*, the wisdom to *understand*, and the courage to *witness* to the truth of His Holy Word.

APPENDIX

THE MEANING OF "FOREKNEW" IN ROMANS 8:29

"For those whom he foreknew he also predestined to be conformed to the image of his Son, in order that he might be the first-born among many brethren. And those whom he predestined he also called; and those whom he called he also justified; and those whom he justified he also glorified." Romans 8:29,30

Broadly speaking there have been two general views as to the meaning and use of the word "foreknew" in Romans 8:29. One class of commentators (the Arminians) maintain that Paul is saying that God predestined to salvation those whom He *foreknew* would respond to His offer of grace (i.e., those whom He saw would of their own free will repent of their sins and believe the gospel). Godet, in commenting on Romans 8:29, asks the question: "In what respect did God thus *foreknow* them?" and answers that they were "foreknown as sure to fulfill the conditions of salvation, viz. *faith;* so: foreknown as His *by faith.*"[1] The word "foreknew" is thus understood by the Arminians to mean that God knew beforehand which sinners would believe, etc., and on the basis of this knowledge He predestined them unto salvation.

The other class of commentators (the Calvinists) reject the above view on two grounds. First, because the Arminians' interpretation is not in keeping with the meaning of Paul's language and second, because it is out of harmony with the system of doctrine taught in the rest of the Scriptures. Calvinists contend that the passage teaches that God set His heart upon (i.e., foreknew) certain individuals; these He predestined or marked out to be saved. Notice that the text does *not* say that God *knew* SOMETHING ABOUT *particular individuals* (that they would do this or that), but it states that God *knew the individuals* THEMSELVES —those whom He *knew* He predestined to be made like Christ. The word "foreknew" as used here is thus understood to be equivalent to "foreloved"—those who were the objects of God's love, He marked out for salvation.

The questions raised by the two opposing interpretations are these: Did God look down through time and see that certain individuals would believe and thus predestine them unto salvation on the basis of this foreseen faith? Or did God set His heart on certain individuals and because of His love for them predestine that they should be called and given faith in Christ by the Holy Spirit and thus be saved? In other words, is the individual's faith the *cause* or the *result* of God's predestination?

---

[1] Frederic Godet, *Commentary on the Epistle to the Romans*, p. 325. Italics are his.

A. The meaning of "foreknew" in Romans 8:29

God has always possessed perfect knowledge of all creatures and of all events. There has never been a time when anything past, present, or future was not fully known to Him. But it is not His knowledge of future events (of what people would do, etc.) which is referred to in Romans 8:29,30, for Paul clearly states that those whom He *foreknew* He predestined, He called, He justified, etc. Since all men are *not* predestined, called, and justified, it follows that all men were *not foreknown* by God in the sense spoken of in verse 29.

It is for this reason that Arminians are forced to add some qualifying notion. They read into the passage some idea not contained in the language itself such as those whom He foreknew *would believe etc.*, He predestined, called, and justified. But according to the Biblical usage of the words "know," "knew," and "foreknew" there is not the least need to make such an addition, and since it is unnecessary, it is improper. When the Bible speaks of God knowing particular individuals, it often means that He has special regard for them, that they are the objects of His affection and concern. For example in Amos 3:2, God, speaking to Israel says, "You only have I known of all the families of the earth; therefore I will punish you for all your iniquities." The Lord knew *about* all the families of the earth, but He knew Israel in a special way. They were His chosen people whom He had set His heart upon. See Deuteronomy 7:7,8; 10:15. Because Israel was His in a special sense He chastised them, cf. Hebrews 12:5,6. God, speaking to Jeremiah, said, "Before I formed you in the womb, I knew you," (Jeremiah 1:5). The meaning here is not that God knew *about* Jeremiah but that He had special regard for the prophet before He formed him in his mother's womb. Jesus also used the word "knew" in the sense of personal, intimate awareness. "On that day many will say to me, 'Lord, Lord, did we not prophesy in your name, and cast out demons in your name, and do many mighty works in your name?' And then will I declare to them, 'I never knew you; depart from me, you evildoers' " (Matt. 7:22,23). Our Lord cannot be understood here as saying, I knew nothing about you, for it is quite evident that He knew all too much about them—their evil character and evil works; hence, His meaning must be, I never knew you intimately nor personally, I never regarded you as the objects of my favor or love. Paul uses the word in the same way in I Corinthians 8:3, "But if one loves God, one is *known* by him," and also II Timothy 2:19, "the Lord knows those who are His." The Lord knows *about* all men but He only *knows* those "who love Him, who are called according to His purpose" (Rom. 8:28)—*those who are His!*

Murray's argument in favor of this meaning of "foreknew" is very good. "It should be observed that the text says '*whom* he foreknew'; *whom* is the object of the verb and there is no qualifying addition. This, of itself, shows that, unless there is some other compelling reason, the expression 'whom he foreknew' contains within itself the differentiation which is presupposed. If the apostle had in mind some 'qualifying adjunct' it would have been simple to supply it. Since he adds none we are forced to inquire if the actual terms he uses can express the differentiation implied. The usage of Scripture provides an affirmative answer. Although the term 'foreknew' is used seldom in the New Testament, it is altogether indefensible to ignore the meaning so frequently given to the word 'know' in the usage of Scripture; 'foreknow' merely adds the thought of 'beforehand' to the word 'know'. Many times in Scripture 'know' has a pregnant meaning which goes beyond that of mere cognition. It is used in a sense practically synonymous with 'love', to set regard upon, to know with peculiar interest, delight, affection, and action (cf. Gen. 18:19; Exod. 2:25; Psalm 1:6; 144:3; Jer. 1:5; Amos 3:2; Hosea 13:5; Matt. 7:23; I Cor. 8:3; Gal. 4:9; II Tim. 2:19; I John 3:1). There is no reason why this import of the word 'know' should not be applied to 'foreknow' in this passage, as also in 11:2 where it also occurs in the same kind of construction and where the thought of election is patently present (cf. 11:5,6). When this import is appreciated, then there is no reason for adding any qualifying notion and 'whom he foreknew' is seen to contain within itself the differentiating element required. It means 'whom he set regard upon' or 'whom he knew from eternity with distinguishing affection and delight' and is virtually equivalent to 'whom he foreloved'. This interpretation, furthermore, is in agreement with the efficient and determining action which is so conspicuous in every other link of the chain—it is God who predestinates, it is God who calls, it is God who justifies, and it is he who glorifies. Foresight of faith would be out of accord with the determinative action which is predicated of God in these other instances and would constitute a weakening of the total emphasis at the point where we should least expect it . . . . It is not the foresight of difference but the foreknowledge that makes difference to exist, not a foresight that recognizes existence but the foreknowledge that determines existence. It is a sovereign distinguishing love."[2]

Hodge observes that "as *to know* is often *to approve* and *love*, it may express the idea of peculiar affection in this case; or it may mean to *select* or *determine upon* . . . . The usage of the word is favourable to either modification of this general idea *of preferring*. 'The people which he foreknew,' i.e., loved or selected, Rom. 11:2; 'Who verily was foreordained (Gr. *foreknown*), i.e., *fixed upon, chosen* before the foundation of the world,' I Peter 1:20; II Tim. 2:19; John 10:14,15; see also Acts 2:23; I Peter 1:2. The idea, therefore, obviously is, that those whom God peculiarly loved, and by thus loving, distinguished or selected from the rest of mankind; or to express both ideas in one word, those whom *he elected* he predestined, etc."[3]

---

[2] John Murray, *The Epistle to the Romans*, Vol. I, pp. 316-318. Italics are his.
[3] Charles Hodge, *Commentary on the Epistle to the Romans*, pp. 283, 284. Italics are his.

Although God knew *about* all men before the world began, He did not *know* all men in the sense that the Bible sometimes uses the word "know," i.e., with intimate personal awareness and love. It is in this latter sense that God foreKNEW those whom He predestined, called, and justified, as outlined in Romans 8:29, 30!

B. Romans 8:29 does not refer to the foresight of faith, good works, etc.

As was pointed out above, it is unnecessary and therefore indefensible to add any qualifying notion such as faith to the verb foreknew in Romans 8:29. The Arminians make this addition, not because the language requires it, but because their theological system requires it— they do it to escape the doctrines of unconditional predestination and election. They *read* the notion of foreseen faith *into* the verse and then appeal to it in an effort to prove that predestination was based on foreseen events. Thus particular individuals are said to be saved, *not* because *God willed* that they should be saved (for He willed the salvation of everyone) *but* because *they themselves willed* to be saved. Hence salvation is made to depend ultimately on the individual's will, not on the sovereign will of Almighty God—faith is understood to be man's gift to God, not God's gift to man.

Haldane, comparing Scripture with Scripture, clearly shows that the foreknowledge mentioned in Romans 8:29 cannot have reference to foreseen faith, good works, or the sinner's response to God's call. "Faith cannot be the cause of foreknowledge, because foreknowledge is before predestination, and faith is the effect of predestination. 'As many as were ordained to eternal life believed,' Acts 13:48. Neither can it be meant of the foreknowledge of good works, because these are the effects of predestination. 'We are His workmanship, created in Christ Jesus unto good works; which God hath before ordained (or before prepared) that we should walk in them;' Eph. 2:10. Neither can it be meant of foreknowledge of our concurrence with the external call, because our effectual calling depends not upon that concurrence, but upon God's purpose and grace, given us in Christ Jesus before the world began, 2 Tim. 1:9. By this foreknowledge, then, is meant, as has been observed, the love of God towards those whom he predestinates to be saved through Jesus Christ. All the called of God are foreknown by Him,—that is, they are the objects of His eternal love, and their calling comes from this free love. 'I have loved thee with an everlasting love; therefore with lovingkindness I have drawn thee,' Jer. 31:3."[4]

Murray, in rejecting the view that "foreknew" in Romans 8:29 refers to the foresight of faith, is certainly correct in stating that "It needs to be emphasized that the rejection of this interpretation is not dictated by a predestinarian interest. Even if it were granted that 'foreknew'

---

[4] Robert Haldane, *Exposition of the Epistle to the Romans*, p. 397.

means the foresight of faith, the biblical doctrine of sovereign election is not thereby eliminated or disproven. For it is certainly true that God foresees faith; he foresees all that comes to pass. The question would then simply be: whence proceeds this faith which God foresees? And the only biblical answer is that the faith which God foresees is the faith he himself creates (cf. John 3:3-8; 6:44, 45, 65; Eph. 2:8; Phil. 1:29; II Pet. 1:2). Hence his eternal foresight of faith is preconditioned by his decree to generate this faith in those whom he foresees as believing, and we are thrown back upon the differentiation which proceeds from God's own eternal and sovereign election to faith and its consequents. The interest, therefore, is simply one of interpretation as it should be applied to this passage. On exegetical grounds we shall have to reject the view that 'foreknew' refers to the foresight of faith."[5]

C. Various ways in which the Greek word "foreknew" (proegno) has been rendered in modern English translations of the New Testament

The root Greek word (proegno) literally translated foreknew and foreknowledge occurs seven times in the Greek New Testament. Twice it refers to previous knowledge on the part of *man:* In Acts 26:5 to the Jews' previous knowledge of Paul, and in II Peter 3:17 to the Christians' previous knowledge (being forewarned) of scoffers who would come in the last days. Five times it refers to *God's* foreknowledge: Three of these times it is used as a verb, Romans 8:29, 11:2; and I Peter 1:20, and twice as a noun, Acts 2:23 and I Peter 1:2. The following quotations show how various modern translations have attempted to convey in English the Biblical connotations of the word when used in reference to *God's* foreknowledge. In each quotation the English word or phrase which corresponds to the Greek word "foreknew" is CAPITALIZED so that the reader may see at a glance how the translators have rendered it. These various renderings certainly show, in the opinion of these translators, that when used in reference to God's foreknowledge in the New Testament, the word connotes more than simple knowledge of future events.[6]

Moffatt's Translation

Rom. 8:29   "For he decreed of old that those whom he PREDESTINED should share the likeness of his Son . . ."

Rom. 11:2   "God has not repudiated his People, his PREDESTINED People!"

---

[5] Murray, *Romans*, Vol. I, p. 316.

[6] See the article on "Foreknow" in the *International Standard Bible Encyclopaedia*, Vol. II, pp. 1128-1131 and *Baker's Dictionary of Theology*, p. 225. See also W. Cunningham, *Historical Theology*, Vol. II, pp. 441-449. Cf. the article on "Predestination" by J. I. Packer in *The New Bible Dictionary*, pp. 1024-1026.

I Pet. 1:2   "whom God the Father has PREDESTINED and chosen, . . ."

I Pet. 1:20   "He was PREDESTINED before the foundation of the world . . ."

Acts 2:23   "this Jesus, betrayed in the PREDESTINED COURSE of God's deliberate purpose, . . ."

Goodspeed's Translation

Rom. 8:29   "For those whom he HAD MARKED OUT FROM THE FIRST he predestined to be made like his Son, . . ."

Rom. 11:2   "God has not repudiated his people, which he HAD MARKED OUT FROM THE FIRST."

I Pet. 1:2   "whom God the Father has chosen and PREDESTINED . . ."

I Pet. 1:20   "who was PREDESTINED for this before the foundation of the world, . . ."

Acts 2:23   "But you, by the fixed purpose and INTENTION of God, handed him over to wicked men, . . ."

Wuest, An Expanded Translation of the New Testament

Rom. 8:29   "Because, those whom He FOREORDAINED He also marked out beforehand . . ."

Rom. 11:2   "God did not repudiate His people whom He FOREORDAINED."

I Pet. 1:2   "chosen-out ones, this choice having been determined by the FOREORDINATION of God the Father . . ."

I Pet. 1:20   "who indeed was FOREORDAINED before the foundation of the universe was laid, . . ."

Acts 2:23   "this One, having been delivered up by the counsel of God which [in the council held by the Trinity] had decided upon His destiny, even by the FOREORDINATION of God WHICH IS THAT ACT FIXING HIS DESTINY, . . ."

Phillips' New Testament

Rom. 11:2   "It is unthinkable that God should have repudiated his own people, the people WHOSE DESTINY HE HIMSELF APPOINTED."

I Pet. 1:2   "whom God the Father KNEW and chose long ago to be made holy by his Spirit, . . ."

I Pet. 1:20   "It is true that God CHOSE him to fulfill his part before the world was founded, . . ."

The Amplified New Testament

Rom. 8:29   "For those whom He FOREKNEW—OF WHOM HE WAS AWARE . . ."

Rom. 11:2   "No, God has not rejected *and* disowned His people [whose destiny] He had MARKED OUT *and* APPOINTED *and* FOREKNOWN FROM THE BEGINNING."

Williams' New Testament

Rom. 8:29   "For those ON WHOM HE SET HIS HEART BEFORE-HAND He marked off as His own to be made like His Son, . . ." Williams gives the following footnote: "Lit., *foreknew* but in Septuagint used as translated."

Rom. 11:2   "No, God has not disowned His people, ON WHOM HE SET HIS HEART BEFOREHAND."

I Pet. 1:20   "who was FOREORDAINED . . ."

The New English Bible

Rom. 8:29   "For God KNEW HIS OWN BEFORE EVEN THEY WERE, and also ordained that they should be shaped to the likeness of his Son, . . ."

Rom. 11:2   "No! God has not rejected the people which he ACKNOWL-EDGED OF OLD AS HIS OWN."

I Pet. 1:2   "chosen of old IN THE PURPOSE of God the Father, . . ."

I Pet. 1:20   "He was PREDESTINED before the foundation of the world, . . ."

Acts 2:23   "When he had been given to you, by the deliberate will and PLAN of God, you used heathen men to crucify and kill him."

D. Conclusion

As was stated at the outset, Calvinists reject the Arminian interpretation of Romans 8:29 on two grounds, (1) because it is not in keeping with the meaning of Paul's language, and (2) because it is out of harmony with the system of doctrine taught in the rest of the Scriptures. This Appendix has been devoted to demonstrating the validity of the first objection. Part II of this work dealt with the latter objection.

INDEX OF PERSONS

INDEX OF SCRIPTURES QUOTED